A GaWaNi Pony Boy Book

# OF WOMEN AND HORSES

## *More Expressions of the Magical Bond*

A New Collection of Essays by Horsewomen

With Commentary by GaWaNi Pony Boy

Illustrations by Various Artists – Photographs by Mark J. Barrett

BowTie Press®
A Division of BowTie, Inc.
Irvine, California

Karla Austin, *Business Operations Manager*
Nick Clemente, *Special Consultant*
Ruth Strother and Jarelle S. Stein, *Editors*
Jennifer Perumean, *Assistant Editor*
Jill Dupont, *Production*
Bocu & Bocu, *Book Design*

Text copyright © 2005 by BowTie Press®
Photographs © Mark J. Barrett, www.markjbarrett.com
Additional images courtesy of: **1, 48, 114, 116, 120, 162:** © Lesley Harrison. **3, 29 (top), 47 (top), 62 (top),
85 (top), 99 (top), 121 (top), 139, 155, 171, 187:** © GaWaNi Pony Boy, www.ponyboy.com **6, 10, 42, 56, 86, 88,
100, 134, 165:** © Dawn Trinkler. **12:** © Alex Layos. **17, 103, 105:** © Photos by Cappy Jackson. **18, 140, 143, 176:**
© Katie Upton. **20, 21, 23:** © Chigga Miller. **47 (bottom), 61, 77, 90, 92–93, 113, 128, 156, 192:** © Liliana
Gomez. **24, 26, 27:** © Kim McElroy. **29 (bottom), 30, 52, 54–55:** © Cheri Sorensen. **32, 36:** © Carol Harris. **37, 50:**
© Shawna Karrasch. **38, 40, 41, 78:** © Karmel Timmons. **58:** Debbie Dolan-Sweeney. **66:** © Sylvia Loch. **74:** © Julie
Goodnight. **81:** © Lola Michelin. **96–98, 125, 153, 170, 186:** © Margo McKnight. **103, 105:** © Lynn Palm. **109,
111:** © Pat Roberts. **124:** © Peggy Cummins. **132, 133:** © Karen Brenner. **136:** © Saret Tola. **144, 146, 147, 185:**
© Heidi Harner. **150:** © Lisa Colombe. **159:** © 2003 by Randi Muster. **161:** © 2003 by Ewell and Ketcham.
**164:** © Melissa Holbrook Pierson. **168:** © Anna-Jane White-Mullin. **174:** © Kathy Hawkins.
**178–181:** © Cali Caberra. **184:** © Rachel Allgyer.

Library of Congress Cataloging-in-Publication Data

Of women and horses : more expressions of the magical bond : a new
collection of essays / by Horsewomen ; with commentary by GaWaNi Pony Boy.
    p. cm.
  ISBN 1-931993-35-1
  1. Horsemen and horsewomen—Psychology. 2. Horses—Psychological
aspects. 3. Human-animal relationships. I. Pony Boy, GaWaNi, 1965- II. Title.

SF284.5.O46 2005
636.1'001'9—dc22

2005009625

BowTie Press®
A Division of BowTie, Inc.
3 Burroughs
Irvine, California 92618

Printed and bound in Thailand
10 9 8 7 6 5 4 3 2 1

*In Memory of Mary Dann:*
*Western Shoshone Grandmother*

# Contents

# Foreword

*"You took me to adventure and to love. We two have shared great joy and great sorrow. And now I stand at the gate of the paddock watching you run in an ecstasy of freedom, knowing you will return to stand quietly, loyally, beside me."*

—Pam Brown, Author

*Sharing a relationship with a horse creates an opportunity for a woman's personal discovery and expansion. Connections made between horses and women are composed of multiple layers. The deepest layers are nonverbal and difficult to express because they touch the deepest part of the human spirit. Many animals, including domestic pets, offer us a similarly layered bonding, yet the equine-human relationship is unique. The horse, with its ability to carry a rider, provides a woman with an opportunity for unequaled collaborative effort. This collaboration creates progressively rich experiences that can powerfully affect a woman's life.*

*Harmony is the element instantly recognizable in the bond shared by women and horses, and it is the final goal of any equine endeavor. Bonding with a horse gives the gift of balance to a woman's life: physical, emotional, and spiritual. The unspoken communication, which serves as therapy in the form of touch between woman and horse, can open her heart and heal her body and mind. Balance is the target of every key area of human life, and by working toward this goal with a horse, a woman can achieve harmony that benefits all relationships. For relationships are the canvas of our lives, and because women are primarily involved in the cultural tradition of creating and preserving familial bonds, women are truly able to understand the transforming potential of a life with horses.*

*As in the previous volume (*Of Women and Horses*), within these pages horsewomen share their personal stories about bonding with horses and talk about the many ways that connection has enriched their lives. Some of them have been inspired to express their love for horses in art, which can also been found throughout this book. Whether rendered in words or in a painting, the balanced picture of a woman and horse in harmony is itself a work of art, visually stunning and lyrically complete.*

—Chaia King

# Introduction

*Like human beings, horses are all individuals with singular personalities, their own virtues and their own faults. We become bound to them for their beauty, their eccentricities, their heart and the love they so often return to us.*

—Lana Slaton, *Horses in History Coloring Album*

*How many times have we looked at women and their horses? In my line of work, I see them almost daily. Yet not until I began an exploration of this profound relationship did I know about the hidden parts of the connection between women and horses. Several years ago, I began a literary journey writing the first book titled* Of Women and Horses. *Writing this first book taught me a lot about horses and a few things about women. The unseen relationship between them is stronger than the obvious attraction that almost any girl can tell you about. Words such as* empowerment, balance, self-esteem, *and* liberation *are commonly used by horsewomen to describe what they purchase from their horses. They purchase these attributes with their own love and nurturing from animals some people might assume would do just fine without them. Not so.*

*After constructing this book and its predecessor, I am convinced that the horse needs women as much as women need the horse. Is there any other animal who could provide for women what the horse does? I don't believe that there is. If I stop and think about all in the animal kingdom, I cannot think of one single creature here on Earth who could even come close to filling the void that would be present if there were no horses.*

*The relationship between women and horses is not only about what horses get from women or what women get from horses. The relationship is about a balance that exists in the universe between these two animals, the woman and the horse. Somehow, for some reason, these two animals stand on opposite ends of a seesaw; in doing so, they keep the people around them in balance as well. This is not a scientifically proven fact, and it has not been published in medical or psychological journals, but there are very few people more qualified than I to make this sort of statement. The people who are more qualified are peers and friends, and they would agree with me.*

*Women and horses work in harmony with each other. We tend to view other symbiotic relationships to be only those that have direct tangible effects on each other, effects that can be easily seen or touched. Could the universe continue on its course if women did not have horses or if horses did not have women? Many of the women in this book would say no, and I would tend to agree with them. I don't think that we need to know the intricacies of a symbiotic relationship to believe that it exists.*

*Try, for a moment, to imagine what the world would be like without horses. Next, try to think about your favorite horsewoman and who or what she would be like if horses were not a part of her life. I have tried this several times, and my imagination is not able to comprehend these women without the horse. I can't imagine which domestic animal would take the horse's place. Where would my own daughter be without her horses? She certainly would not be the caring, powerful, balanced young woman she has turned out to be. It bothers me deeply to think about a world without horses and the balance that they provide. I am thankful that God has provided us with the horse.*

# MADE FOR ETERNITY

*by Alexandra Layos*

*Horses and children,*
*I often think, have a lot of the good*
*sense there is in the world.*

—Josephine Demott Robinson (1865–1948),
*The Circus Lady*

# Looking back now

on my seventeen years, I can't help but feel grateful for all of the horses with which my life has been blessed. Since I was a few months old, they have come and gone, each teaching me something in the process. From my first pony to my five-gaited saddlebred to the tiny Morgan who changed my world, each has brought me to a deeper understanding of the connection that exists between humans and horses.

Horses posses a powerful spirit; there is a brilliance about them, emanating from their beings. They are the epitome of beauty and grace, and these characteristics, coupled with their strength and kindness, are what attract people to them. Powerful teachers, horses are constantly changing lives for the better, teaching people how to be better humans through a deeper connection to and understanding of nature.

It is this special connection that makes great riders. Once the rider moves beyond the physical and accepts that controlling the horse's energy is more important, a true partnership can be achieved. Riding becomes more precise; the unseen signals become the most important; it turns into a mental game instead of a physical one.

The intuitive nature of these creatures is simply incredible. I've watched so-called difficult horses sense a young or insecure rider and immediately drop down to her level. I've watched the same horse perform three different ways depending on who was in the saddle.

There are many times when horses understand more than we do. My first saddlebred, Super Town, was a retired five-gaited horse in his twenties when I owned him. I remember taking short trail rides on him around the farm when I was about eight years old. I'll never forget the time I asked him to walk along the far fence line and he refused. I insisted. He backed up and snorted nervously. "Super!" I scolded, pressing him forward with my heels. Finally, he walked toward the bottom of the hill by the fence and immediately sank up to his fetlocks in mud. I was lucky he didn't pull a shoe or hurt himself while scrambling to get out. After that, I always listened to what he was trying to tell me.

Super Town was also the horse I rode one-handed while recuperating from an accident (severing the radial nerve in my right arm) that left me without the use of my hand for close to a year. He was an angel, walking and even trotting slowly around the arena whenever I asked, although he'd never been ridden western in his life and didn't

have a clue how to neck-rein. Somehow he followed a combination of my legs and thoughts and my attempts at direct-rein using only my left hand. Although in his twenties, he still loved to rack, yet he moseyed along at a walk simply because I asked him to. He knew that there was something different about me during those months—that I needed him to behave and be the angel who kept me in the saddle against the wishes of all my doctors.

The bonds existing between horses and their owners run much deeper than most people realize. I know horses who get upset with their owners when they are away on vacation or even when they simply miss a ride or two. When the rider eventually does show up, these horses turn away or behave very badly during the ride, as if to say, "I'm upset with you, where were you?" They get over it after a bit, but it shows just how much our relationship means to our equine friends.

The concept of a little girl and her horse is timeless. Almost every young girl has dreamed about getting a pony for her birthday or riding into the sunset on a big black stallion of her own. The romantic notions of freedom and the power felt on horseback are initially the captivating factors of this fascination, even for the youngest of girls. Yet once a real horse comes into the picture, many other reasons for loving the horse are added. Because of their

innocence, their true desire to learn, to understand, and to know, girls connect so well with horses. If horses are anything, they are teachers, and girls are open to their lessons. Young girls haven't yet been told that communicating with a horse is dumb or crazy or stupid or impossible. Their openness and willingness to trust what they're receiving from the animals allow horses to reach out and touch girls in a very special way.

Ralph Waldo Emerson said of self-trust, "These are the voices which we hear in solitude, but they grow faint and inaudible as we enter into the world." The world has a habit of pushing people away from self-trust. So the millions of young girls who began with a birthday pony grow up. The voices have a habit of growing "faint and inaudible" as one grows, but they don't have to. For many women, a connection continues to exist between themselves and their horses. For those who find themselves drawn as adults to these majestic creatures, this connection is still possible, since horses have a habit of getting humans to continually open up to them.

I have experienced this deep connection with almost all of the horses in my life, but my greatest human-horse relationship began when I was eleven years old, with a Morgan named Astonishinglee. We called him Leroy. He was a clown, a ham, and

so much more, and it was on his back that I learned to really ride. With every graceful stride he took, he challenged me. He was the master at being difficult, whether he was shying, bucking, spinning, or just going from a show trot to a dead halt in the matter of two seconds for no apparent reason. He was a champion already, well known in the show world. I couldn't let him down. I had to rise up, take control, stay with him, and let him be the champion that he was. If for one second I didn't meet his challenges, he was off playing his games again. He was certainly not going to compensate for my mistakes! In the end, he taught me to do it his way, and his way was riding the mind of the horse, not just his body.

When I looked into his eyes, everything was all right. He was my greatest friend, and I adored him. But more than that, I was "his girl." I'll never forget the year my trainer left balloons on Leroy's stall door for my birthday. When I arrived, he raced to the front of the stall excitedly and whinnied loudly, as if he'd been waiting all day for that moment to wish me a happy birthday. I spent every moment I could in his stall; we shared time together as any good friends would. I held conversations with him, read him stories, and even took naps with him. We looked at magazines together; I taught him tricks. He was the friend that I had looked for all of my life; he just happened to come in the form of a horse.

For two happy years we were together, then fate took him away. His mystery illness was the talk of all the vets. No one could diagnose it. He fought for months and eventually beat it. The vets twisted his name around to celebrate his victory, calling him Amazinglee. But his heart had weakened from the struggle. He remained with us for one last happy Christmas, then took his leave on January 10, 2001, at the young age of twelve. Yet I can still feel his presence. He remains my greatest friend, and I remain eternally grateful for his lessons and his part in my life, for the many new friends I have come to know through him, and for my renewed faith. Our lives were intricately interwoven for a reason.

His story has become somewhat of a legend in the years since his passing. The first time people hear it, they hear a tragic tale of loss, a story of a brave little horse and the people who loved him. Then they listen to it a few more times and begin to see the truth, the real nature of Leroy, his purpose in our lives even now. They hear the story from the people who were there, who watched his dancing eyes, who witnessed his heroic battle, and who saw him win it. Then they see that there is more, so much more, for he has shaped my life like no other has or probably ever will.

After all these years, I've barely begun to grasp the depths of this connection. I close my eyes and see Leroy standing with the other friends I've lost along the way. Yet I know he is still here with me, and my life is made richer for this knowledge.

What can I really say about the relationship between women and their horses? Put simply, it is that this friendship is one made in and for eternity. For me, this is an eternity that begins here on earth and will continue in the place where my equine friends, led by Leroy, are patiently awaiting me. Those of you who have been lucky enough to truly know a horse understand these words; to those of you who haven't yet found that special connection, my wish is for you to experience it at least once in your lifetime. Once is all you need—it will change you forever.

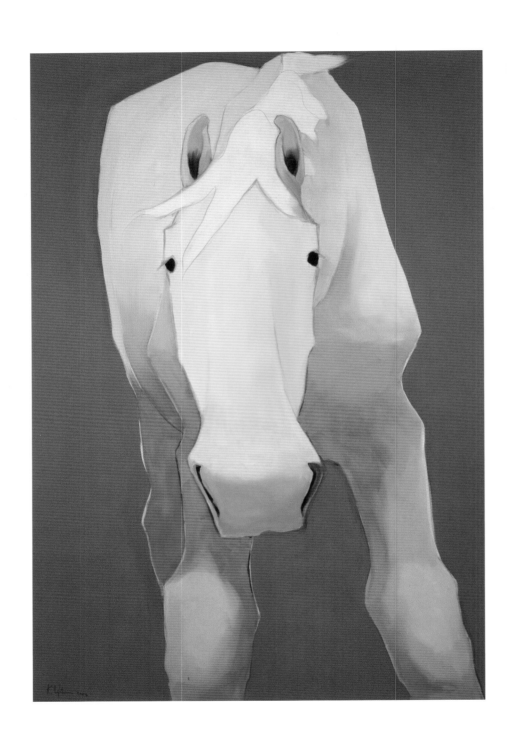

# A TWO-HORSE WOMAN AND
# A TWO-WOMAN HORSE

*by Linda "Chigger" Miller*

*The wildest colts*
*only make the best horses.*

—Plutarch (AD 46–120),
*Life of Themistocles*

# When I moved from

southwest Missouri to east Tennessee with my husband and two children in 1976, I was so homesick for family that for the first year I could think only of going back home. Then I met T. A. Robertson, a very special person. A mutual friend who happened to be one of his riding buddies introduced us. T. A. had been Dolly Parton's first grade teacher, and even though he had retired from teaching, he was still called in to substitute once in a while. T. A. often rode Goldie, his mare, to school, and she would patiently wait for him under the cool shade of the trees on the front lawn. It wasn't hard to spot the days he was working. He was about seventy years old at that time, and luckily for me he still wanted to teach.

Where I grew up, there were a few grade horses and a few Missouri fox-trotters around, although I never had the opportunity to ride one. Most of my experience was riding workhorses because my father used them to plow. T. A. introduced me to the Tennessee walking horse. It was love at first ride! I did not know anything about the gaits or much about horses in general, but I knew that I loved to ride.

Those days were so special because T. A. still was a teacher at heart and wanted to share his seventy years of knowledge about horses. He had ridden horses since he was old enough to sit atop one, and he still believed there was much more that he could learn from the horse. We rode twenty miles or more four or five times a week. He meant for me to learn, and I was like a sponge trying to soak in all that he had to say. I'll bet that I mouthed every horse in the county until T. A. was satisfied that I could accurately age a horse by his teeth. T. A. had many stories and so much information to tell

about horse behavior, and several stories about the mischievous side of Dolly as a first grader. He kept me spellbound every day we rode together.

After the passing of T. A., I felt an obligation to his memory to pass along as much of his years of experience and knowledge as I could. I started teaching basic riding and horse care. One thing that I learned on my own and believe in strongly is that riding and horse care go together, and you should not teach one without the other. It isn't fair to your students or to the horses.

By this time, I had about eight horses I felt could be used to teach lessons safely. One of these was a small black mare named Sugar who was as quick as a rabbit. She would come back from a twenty-mile mountain ride as hyper as when she had left. She unloaded some of my friends and me

a time or two, and she was like a mad hornet in the field with other horses. For that reason, we kept her in the barn most of the time.

Sugar was especially hateful at mealtime. As soon as she heard the feed cans rattle, she would pin her ears back and start violently kicking the walls of the stall. I tried feeding her first, last, not at all, and even in different places on the farm. Nothing seemed to convince her that she really did not have to be so angry. Once the food had been put into her bucket, she would calm down somewhat and eat in peace. Even then, the slightest noise could still cause her to kick the walls. Although I really did not like that behavior, I could not change it. So I simply resigned myself to making sure no one was around her during feeding time.

Despite her attitude at meal times, Sugar could be as sweet as any other horse in the arena when she had a youngster on her back. Time after time, she would let the students clean her feet and never showed any signs of bad behavior. They would mount and dismount many times—nearside and offside mounts. Sugar was always fine with all that. I kept a close eye on her, anyway.

I owned Sugar for quite some time and used her in many lessons until Jessica, a twelve-year-old student, wanted to ride Sugar every lesson. She was the only student who would give Sugar a huge hug when she arrived and again after the lesson. Most of the students would try to leave without the required cooldown grooming, but not Jessica. She would have stayed all night with that horse if her mom had allowed it. She was a natural rider and very well balanced. Jessica and Sugar made a great team, and I knew that it wouldn't be long before Jessica would want Sugar for her very own.

I really was reluctant to think about selling Sugar because of her habits at mealtime. Jessica loved the little mare, and this mare was especially careful with Jessica. Anyone could see that she and Jessica had an unexplainable bond. Sugar would recognize her and nicker each time she came into the barn. Their personalities were even somewhat the same. They were true kindred spirits. Jessica was trusting with Sugar and Sugar's nasty side while she ate. How could I say no?

Jessica owned Sugar for about six years and then had to go away to college. She was so upset because she no longer had time to spend with Sugar. She felt that it was unfair to ask Sugar to be confined to a stall and wait for her. Jessica was most upset at the thought of selling Sugar to someone she did not know and who might sell her again if things did not work out, which often happens. I could feel and see the anxiety in Jessica. She wanted the best for Sugar—happy days and a secure home with a lot of love. She made a very grown-up decision for a teenage girl, but it took all of her courage.

I decided to purchase Sugar from Jessica and return her to lessons. She wasn't the same mare. You could tell that her best friend and soul mate had left, and it had broken Sugar's heart. Jessica's heart was grieving, too, but she knew that she had made the right decision. It was quite a while before Sugar returned to her frisky self. Even then, she did not have that special sparkle in her eyes. She watched everyone who came to the barn but nickered at no one.

Occasionally, I rode Sugar again on the trail, but she just wasn't the same. I felt so sorry for her that the next decision wasn't hard at all. I decided to have her bred. Right or wrong, I guess that I was hoping a foal would take the place of Jessica for a while.

Ironically, within a month, friends wanted to find a horse for their daughter, Katherine. Her birthday was just around the corner, and she asked about Sugar. Katherine was only ten years old and had no fear of horses. I mean absolutely none. Sugar was older and awaiting the foal when Katherine started lessons with her. It was unbelievable the way the two took to each other. Katherine's parents had several horses at that time. From being at their farm, I knew that Sugar would get the best of care. But the greatest thing was that she would probably have a home with Katherine forever. The sale was made and they took Sugar to their farm.

I had warned them time and time again not to allow Katherine to go into the stall or even be around Sugar when she was eating. Just months after getting Sugar, disaster struck. Sugar kicked Katherine's new puppy and killed it; unfortunately, she saw it happen.

Yet Katherine still trusted Sugar and her faith in Sugar had not waned. She loved her and forgave her.

Katherine has a magic rapport and a connection with horses that only a few experience. I have witnessed things Katherine has done with Sugar that I felt no one could ever have accomplished. For example, Sugar would carry empty five-gallon buckets (four of them tied with hay strings), and they would be dangling around her neck and clanging and bumping around her legs as Katherine was perched bareback. She would sit for hours on the mare in the pasture while Sugar grazed with no halter, bridle, or saddle—just love and trust between the two. After Sugar's colt, Pepper, was born, she shared her most private time with Katherine. Amazingly, during Sugar's feeding times, Katherine could go into the stall and groom her, pick her hooves, and even back her away from the grain. The sparkle back in Sugar's eyes told the whole story. She had a new soul mate.

Katherine rides show horses now, but she still has Sugar. While she is riding other horses, Sugar nickers at her as if to say, "My turn next." In 2003, Katherine Ramsbottom won the youth/owner/amateur (12–17 years) World Grand Championship on her Tennessee walking mare, Pusher's Special Design. She is such an accomplished rider, and I am so very proud of the way in which she shows and treats her horses. You can just see that she is having the most exciting time of her life—both in and out of the show ring. When she rides Sugar in the pasture, she has that same smile that she had when winning the WGC class. Sugar is a World Champion to her, also.

I do believe that women are more capable than men of giving love to a horse. It may be that we think the horse loves us back. Is there really

any harm in that? I think that horses learn to trust women sooner than they do men because horses respond to kindness, gentleness, and most of all to nurturing. This is something that women sort of come by naturally.

Women are eager to be educated on horse behavior and learn how to make sure that they become the horse's "mom," or herd leader. I believe women try to think before acting with their horses because of their respect for such strong, large, and excitable animals. I want to think that trust is really the basis for the relationships that I have seen. The special ones—the connected ones—seem to have something more.

I have had more than a hundred horses since those early days, and I can say that I have ridden enough miles to have circled the earth. I have enjoyed the feeling of protecting and placing horses where I felt they might be that kindred spirit to someone else. I myself have felt this real sort of mind and heart connection with only two horses: Little Man, a golden palomino, and Miss Williams, a chestnut mare. I feel an acceptance, a respect, and a trust from them. Once we women feel that connection with our horses, we want to call it love. I love my horses!

Jessica graduated from college and bought Sugar's colt from Katherine, who continues to ride world champion walking horses. I, along with my husband, am now in a business with Dolly Parton in her Dixie Stampedes, where we entertain millions of horse lovers with horses during dinner shows.

T. A. Robertson is gone now, but Jessica, Katherine, Dolly, and I—and probably Sugar and her colt, Pepper; Little Man; and Miss Williams—are his kindred spirits. Somehow, we are all connected. Maybe that is why God made horses: so we could all be connected in spirit.

"Attraction"

# THE ANCIENT CALL

*by Kim McElroy*

*Four things greater than all things are,*
*Women and Horses and Power and War.*

—Rudyard Kipling (1865–1936),
"The Ballad of the King's Jest"

# Some girls hear

the ancient call to seek out the horse at such an early age that they do not question it; they only know that they must be with horses. Some awaken at adolescence and confound their parents with their sudden interest in all things horse. Others do not become aware of the quest until they become women. They begin to realize that some integral part of them is missing, and through searching find that the horse is the key. Love of horses is something that blooms unbidden in the heart and blossoms even if it is never encouraged to grow.

Women's longing for horses is in some ways akin to the age-old desire in men to be at sea. It is a longing that is powerful but intangible: an equal mix of the desire to be one with horses and to be challenged by them. It is a passion and a quest for fulfillment. It is a need to be empowered by natural forces so that we can define and expand our awareness of our inner selves.

It is interesting to note that in Greek mythology, it is Poseidon, the god of the sea, who created the first horse. Horses and the sea have much in common. Both are beautiful, powerful, and unpredictable. They inspire us, and so we seek the answers to their elusive mysteries. Yet, just as the call of the sea to men remains a mystery, so, too, does the call of horses to a woman's heart remain the subject of much debate.

My path to horses began in early childhood. Like most children, before I could read or write, I drew pictures as a way to express what I felt. Horses were my most common subject matter. When I began to play horse, as girls often do, I imagined I was the horse, not the rider. I wanted to be a horse, and the more I drew horses the more

I was able to escape into that fantasy of being like them. There was no explanation for my love of horses. We lived in the suburbs; horses were not a reality in my world. Yet somehow, somewhere I was awakened to them, and from that moment on they fascinated me.

This longing for horses continued throughout my childhood. My parents sought an answer to my endless requests for a horse by enrolling me in riding lessons, but I quickly discovered that the athletic pursuit of learning how to direct the horse was intimidating and only made me feel more separate from them. I think at a deep level I wanted them to guide me, not the other way around.

Perhaps if I had grown up in a world of open farmland and pastured horses, I might have embraced riding as a way to go together with the

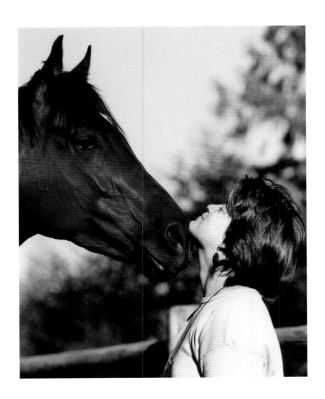

horse to a longed-for destination. Then we would have had the same goal: companionship and escape from the mundane world. But riding in an arena didn't accomplish this feeling of communion. My art continued to be the only outlet for the deep emotional connection I desired.

At the age of eight, I drew a profile of a horse's head superimposed with the image of a woman's face. They were one being, sharing the same eye. This was one of my early artistic attempts to define the concept of oneness with horses, the oneness that I had not been able to find in the real world.

As I grew up and pursued my art studies in college, I lost the theme of horses in my art. I focused on drawing the subjects that my art teachers directed in projects and assignments and perfected the techniques that would ensure that I had the training to round out my talent. But I don't think I really had a passion for art because I didn't know what I wanted to draw.

One year during spring break, I was visiting with a family friend named Geska who owned Arabian horses. I had a project for school to fill up my sketchbook so I decided to draw the horses. I did a few sketches of them standing in their stalls, but the routine drawings didn't inspire me. I still had a love for horses, but I had grown so far away from them that I had forgotten my childhood dreams.

Later that afternoon, Geska let two of the horses out to run in the arena. Watching their dynamic movements was so inspiring I decided to take on the challenge of drawing them in motion using a style of quick gesture sketches I had been learning. After several pages of attempts I became frustrated that I could not capture their fleeting movements on paper. I stopped and I became aware of how disconnected I felt from the horses. I was so busy trying to draw them accurately that I wasn't feeling anything. I realized I didn't want to just watch the horses, I wanted to feel them, to *become* them as I had as a child. I wanted to feel as dynamic and playful and powerful as they were.

As I came to this realization, I took a deep breath and began sketching again. This time I imagined I was the horse, and somehow I drew that feeling on the paper. My mind's eye didn't have to remember their movements because the movements were feelings, not forms. After a few moments I looked back at the sketches, and I instantly knew that something new had happened

in my work, and within myself. The sketches were different than anything I had ever done before. They were dynamic drawings of horses, which had a life of their own.

In this way, horses awakened me to their presence again, and from that time on I painted horses exclusively. As I began to sell my artwork, I found that it was primarily women who responded to my art. I realized this was because other women feel the way I do about horses. Somehow, my intuitive connection with horses allows me to portray them as the dynamic physical, emotional, and spiritual creatures that they are. This is how women long to experience the horse: as a feeling, not just a form; as a consciousness, not just a mind; as a being, not just an animal.

Upon viewing one of my paintings the other day, a woman commented that it made her feel as if she were the horse. She said this with a note of astonishment; the idea of connecting in this way with another being was new to her. This kind of awakening was exactly what I had gone through. Always horses have been my guides.

Years ago I read a book about the differences between men and women. The author believes spirituality comes to women naturally, whereas men perform rituals to experience spirituality. I think this explains the connection between women and horses. At some level, women have an intuitive longing for a deep kinship with the horse. We seek a relationship where there is no separation, no definition to the limits of mind, heart, and spirit. When women approach horses from this perspective, horses respond because they are naturally spiritual beings themselves, and to them there is no separation.

*Kim brings up an interesting part of my own life* that I have never paralleled with a woman's longing for horses: a man's longing to be at sea. I suffer from this longing, and perhaps someday I will be asked by a well-known billfish tournament winner to contribute to her book exploring the relationship between men and the sea. I would jump at the chance.

I have never been taken seriously by interviewers, especially female interviewers, when they have asked the question, "What is your favorite thing to do?" and I answer, "Go fishing." They usually follow up with something like, "No, really," or "Are you serious?" I guess they expect me to reply, "Go on a trail ride." You should know that I would rather pick rocks or chop wood than go on a trail ride. Why? Because I do not enjoy riding on horses; I enjoy interacting with them. I love to have conversations with horses, I love to learn more and more about horses, I love to learn from horses how to be a better teacher, and I absolutely detest sitting on a horse who is going "somewhere" or doing "something" underneath me.

You would not enjoy going on a trail ride with me, unless you are as fanatical about training as I can be at times. I like to use the actual trail as a point of reference for the horse, a place of comfort and relaxation that the horse is allowed to return to after completing an exercise or a maneuver correctly. The last thing that the trail is for me is the planned route.

Back out to sea. I have just been challenged by Kim's essay, and I must admit that I could never do what the essayists in this book have done. I posed all of the women in this book the same question that I presented to the essayists in the first Of Women and Horses: What are your thoughts on women and horses? If that famous billfish fisherwoman asked me, "Tell me your thoughts about men and the sea," I could not begin to express the feelings that the sea holds in my heart—primarily because of two words that do not normally find themselves together in a man's brain: express and feelings.

Not unlike the feelings horses bring to women, the sea brings me balance, clarity, oneness, grounding, and a feeling of iyuptala, the Lakota word for "one-with." Thank you, Kim.

# LUCK OR DESTINY?
# PERHAPS A LITTLE OF BOTH

*by Carol Harris*

*No hour of life is lost that
is spent in the saddle.*

—Winston Churchill (1874–1965)

# I'm finally getting

to the point where I don't mind admitting how long I have been active in the horse industry. It's been more than sixty years. Born Carol Holden Agar in 1923, I dreamed of horses as a child. I had a pony named Dickie when I was seven, and at twelve I was given my first horse—a standardbred pacer named Judge Mahoney whom my father won in a poker game. My next horse was a three-gaited saddle horse named Beau Kalarama. I showed him quite a bit, but I was never very well mounted. Through the years I learned to make the best of what I had, to learn all I could, and then to aspire for better.

My family had no interest in horses at all, so as I look back on all that I have learned to enjoy with my horses, I wonder where this natural love of the horse came from. I have met many women over the years who have had that same horsey love affair and have somehow, with no encouragement, made horses their lives. I am merely one of them, and fortunately I was able to fulfill my dreams through many prayers, a great deal of thought, hard work, and a huge desire to associate with the people who loved horses as much as I did.

Actually, nothing was ever made easy for me with horses. When I outgrew my pony, I was "left afoot." My friends had show horses whom they were able to enjoy and have lessons on. After much begging, I did receive riding lessons on school horses before I was sent away at age fourteen to Kent Place and Westover, two horseless boarding schools. At that time I said to myself, "No one can do this to me forever." During the next eight years of boarding school, junior college, and the Art Students League, I rode when I could, planned for the future, got married, and, in between children, started raising horses.

I've owned, shown, raced, and bred many different breeds—saddle horses, standardbreds, Thoroughbreds, hunters, paints, hackney ponies, Arabians, cutters, reiners, western riders, pleasure horses, trail horses, ropers and barrel racers, miniatures, and many fine halter horses. I loved them all. Cutting and reining, I believe, were my favorites, but cutting eventually became too time-consuming: it deprived me of participating in other events. I've had many outstanding winners, which have given me endless thrills.

One of my horses who affectionately comes to mind is Really Rugged, my amazing Thoroughbred stallion. He sired horses, including top racing, reining, western pleasure, huntseaters, and even the Super Horse, Rugged Lark, who excelled in everything. Today, as I reflect, I truly believe Really Rugged was the most underappreciated stallion of his time. Other horses come to mind as well. I'll also never forget Francie's Hat, my Thoroughbred colt whom I sold only to watch him run second in the Kentucky Derby in 1968; or Jay's Sugar Bars, my 1971 Honor Roll Reining Stallion; or beautiful Hollywood Cat, my top cutting mare. I also loved to ride my handsome dun mare, Hollywood Joan,

whom I not only showed competitively at pleasure but also rode to win the East Coast Cutting Horse Championship. I bred or owned four exceptional stallions who consistently turned out winning, versatile halter and performance babies for me year after year, Eternal Too, Eternal Dell, his son Majestic Dell, and Majestic Dell's son Majestic Justice. These four sires not only kept the Grand Champion Halter Trophies coming but also sired endless performance winners as well. Of course, everyone knows my relationship with the one and only Super Horse and Super Horse sire Rugged Lark. He was the great highlight of my life.

Although I thoroughly enjoyed showing, racing, and training young horses, I believe breeding—both horses and dogs, especially whippets and Italian greyhounds—has always been my primary interest. Horse shows, horse races, and dog shows were the competitions that would expose my success or failure. I always tried to keep in mind how hard my dad had worked to make his family comfortable, so I was inclined to be extremely conservative with the funds he had left me in his will. For this reason, I began my horse-breeding program with a courage that would probably horrify every bloodstock specialist in the country.

From the start, I was convinced that breeding top quarter horses was like trying to complete a jigsaw puzzle—only discovering that I must find the one piece to tie everything together. I felt that the most important missing piece was a dominant breeding stallion. A gorgeous individual from a good family was useless if he couldn't pass on his great qualities to his get.

I wanted so badly to breed horses who could do everything, not just look good. I primarily wanted good minds, but since I had a long association with Thoroughbreds, saddlebreds, and beautiful show dogs—animals with pizzazz—long elegant necks with tiny throat latches and beautiful heads were musts. I believed I could have it all—conformation and performance—in one horse, if I could learn how to pick producing lines and combine them properly. I could have halter horses who would ride and performance horses who would halter. Not only that, if my stud was dominant, everything would become easy and less expensive. Best of all, I then would not have to buy such pricy mares.

The puzzle pieces were more convenient to find with my Thoroughbred operation because the Jockey Club provided lists of leading sires and dams weekly with numbers and percentages to help a breeder. The American Quarter Horse Association did not make it so easy, and sometimes it was quite frustrating to have to appraise a quarter horse sire's value since his record or rate of success was never based on percentages. I courageously applied my own strategy much like a detective would go about unraveling a mystery. I read a lot and talked to many successful horsemen, some I didn't even know. I asked owners and trainers about many horses, their breeding and accomplishments, their trainability, their sire and dam lines, and I listened to fascinating stories about all of them. I also often called on my gut feelings when decisions became difficult.

If it sounds like my ambitions were a lot bigger than my pocketbook, they were. At one time my broodmares didn't have a single halter point among them. Whether it was luck or good sense, I'll never know, but this was the route I took to build a successful family of halter and performance horses.

When I moved to Florida in 1963, I used my less-than-first-rate stock to slowly develop what became an amazingly competitive program. Florida in and of itself was inspiring. The weather, the grass, the abundant sunshine were enough to make me realize how hard I had been making life for myself in New Jersey. The foals in my first crop in Florida were three times bigger, sounder, and better than those my mares had produced up north. In Florida, too, my health was improved and my ambition and vision seemed to grow with my horses.

I never forgot my friends from up north. They were the ones I had shown with and learned with. They were the hunter and jumper friends and the quarter horse people whom I had traveled with to many shows. It was with them that I had met numerous successful breeders and trainers, and I can well remember that Dale Wilkenson, a well-known reining/cutting horse trainer, became my most helpful friend. I spent a great deal of time with him and his wife, Lucy, in Ohio, and he patiently attempted to answer my questions about everything. I feared often that I was too green to understand exactly what he was saying. I darn sure watched him though and continued to do the same with every trainer and rider I met and competed with. Spending time with Dale, Matlock Rose, Buster Welch, George Tyler, Shorty Freemen, John Carter, Frank Chapot, Dave Kelly, and Bob and Joan Rost, to name a few, were in my opinion world-class learning experiences. They influenced my thinking as well as my riding, and today I still reflect on their God-given talents, humor, and kindness. They weren't teachers or clinicians, but they were definitely mentors who at that time, I'm sure, never knew it.

Back in the fifties and sixties, we didn't have personal trainers, seminars, or hundreds of articles to help us; maybe a few books were available but nothing like today's countless clinics and the training tips found in videos and magazines.

Today customs are very different. The hunter riders all have trainers to direct them and their horses from start to finish. To me this is quite sad because now there seems to be little room for the development of individual styles, thoughts, and opinions. The trainer is completely in command, and the amateurs and owners have become very much like bewildered soldiers waiting for the next command. Unfortunately, the world of western disciplines seems to be following the same road: trainers are also in command and once again the owners seem content to pay the bills and have their pictures taken. The judges and the trainers are now one and the same, and the poor, unsuspecting owner has let it happen. It appears everybody is permitting the professionals to take over a job the owners should be doing. I predict that our beautiful sport is in for some shaky times because of constant conflicts of interests that develop between owners and trainers.

I try not to think too much about what may happen in the future because the present is more important. I believe, however, that we should look back and reflect on where we've come from. We should try to remember the importance of the early breeders. It is obvious that they held the secrets of bloodlines and results. Without them, the cowboys would have been jobless and training would have been unnecessary. The ranchers, who were the breeders, were the stars, the inspired folks who realized that the success and importance of their ranches relied on the quality and the ability of their horses. After all, no tractor or jeep could cut a cow or hunt for strays in rough terrain. Their horses were essential tools for the ranchers who took great pride in their abilities to create the very best.

Through the years the *Quarter Horse Journal* has been my bible; I did my homework and learned who the great breeders were. I became acquainted with some of them and attended their sales, where I longed to buy their expensive horses. I never did, but still I bought their bloodlines, the best I could afford. I always tried to buy horses who thrilled me so I could feel the excitement but never the pressure. Believe it or not, around 1956 I purchased my first cutting horse over the telephone for $1,500 from a man named Pete Lindsay in Paris, Texas. Pete was honest, and I was lucky. The horse I bought, named Swap Out, was adorable looking, well trained, and—guess what?—he was even sound. I never thought of X-rays or having a vet check. I did get burned a few times on horse deals, but in the long run it probably helped me more than it hurt, and eventually I became very careful about the people with whom I did business.

Years flew by for me and being trusting and a friendly sort, I gradually got to know the entire industry—breeders, owners, trainers, judges, vets, farriers, horse show superintendents, and eventually many officers and staff members of the great American Quarter Horse Association. I seemed to like them all; they impressed me—the good ones, the bad ones, and those in between. Most of all, I acquired many, many friends whom I will always cherish. I don't believe anyone has ever had more fun winning and losing than I, and, best of all, now at age eight-two, I'm still having a blast!

Yes, I left New Jersey in 1963 so I have now lived in Florida for exactly forty-two years. Sometimes I can't believe how lucky I am to have such a nice farm. My precious family lives close to me. I still have seventy or so horses, fifty or sixty dogs, several loyal employees, all kinds of beautiful friends, and so many crazy wonderful memories! Indeed, I have been fortunate, and thanks to my mom and my dad and God, I still am.

On October 26, 2004, I lost my special friend, Rugged Lark. I miss him terribly, and according to the number of condolences I have received, I am not alone. People around the world adored my horse, and their expressions of grief and sympathy helped me understand how blessed we at Bo-Bett were to have loved and enjoyed him for almost twenty-four years.

How can I ever express my gratitude to all the folks who have e-mailed, phoned, sent flowers, letters, and pictures? My home will always be open to every one of you, and Lark's life-size memorial statue in bronze will welcome your visits to his final resting place in Bo-Bett farm in Florida. I only hope God enjoys him as much as we did.

# FROM THE OTHER SIDE OF THE FENCE

*by Karmel Timmons*

*The mare lies down in the grass where
the nest of the skylark is hidden.
Her eyes drink the delicate horizon moving behind
the song. Deep sink the skies, a well of voices.
Her sleep is the vessel of Summer.*

—Vernon Watkins (1906–1967), Welsh poet

# Everything that I

know about horses, I have learned from the other side of the fence. Likewise, it is through being an observer that I have learned about the amazing relationships that women develop with their horses. From this perspective, I have witnessed the commitment of time and energy that women make to work with their horses toward the goal of becoming united with this magnificent creature. My commitment lies in capturing the essence of this animal through my artwork rather than directly with a horse, but that doesn't diminish my connection with horses.

There have been countless instances of women coming up to me in tears because they have been moved by one of my drawings. Most often they see a horse whom they own or have lost, and their connection to that horse runs so deep that they are moved to tears. I suppose that one of the greatest rewards as an artist is to be able to experience how deeply my work has touched someone.

For my part, my period as a horse owner was a catalyst for the life I am living today. When I married Matt, we moved into a log home on some land and followed his dream of buying horses and learning to ride. We took a few lessons, then started buying horses, and soon found ourselves with four horses in the backyard—but none educated enough to be a good beginner's horse. Although I couldn't really ride them, I would spend hours upon hours petting them—feeling their coats, their ears, and the bones in their faces. In hindsight, I see that this was research for what I am doing now. I know what a horse feels like under the skin, what a horse smells like, and what a horse sounds like. When these qualities are captured in artwork, the drawing can be truly great.

I was a passionate artist in high school but quickly lost interest after graduation. It wasn't until fifteen years later, after shooting some photos of our new horses, that I picked up a pencil again to draw. I wanted to sketch our *grulla* mare, my favorite of the group. When I finished the sketch and showed Matt, he was so thrilled with the work that he encouraged me to quit my job and start drawing full time. In a couple of years, he, too, left his job. Now we work together: I draw and Matt frames and takes care of the business side of things. Sadly, when the artwork started really rolling, the reality of this lifestyle, traveling to horse events and art shows, made it necessary for us to sell our horses.

Early on in my career, I had the good fortune of running into a local horsewoman who befriended me and continues to educate me about the intrica-

cies of horsemanship. She follows the vaquero tradition of educating a horse. Many of the drawings I have done of horses in traditional gear are because of my connection with her. I have developed a great respect for this way of educating horses because of its history and the amount of time its followers take to create a finished horse. The horses educated in this manner have layer upon layer of experience before they become a finished bridle horse; therefore they have a certain sense of self that is not often seen in other horses.

When I am working on a drawing, I, too, work in layers. When I first see a photo, I know right away if I will want to draw it. Something about it has to grab me. Once I have had that initial reaction, I pick it apart and make sure that all the artistic elements are present and think about how I might change or add certain things to enhance the drawing. And then, of course, I have my technical horse experts take a look and make sure there are no mistakes in the photo.

I spend many hours working on a piece, and even though I'm working from a photograph, I can add so many things to a drawing that don't exist in the photo, such as better lighting, texture, and feeling. People have always said that there is a "live" quality to my work. And the only explanation that I can give is that it's amazing how much can be seen when you look at something for a very long time. Tiny shapes become textures, and layers of textures become the final drawing. When people see one of my drawings, I want them to feel as though they could touch the horse and feel the fur and the wind blowing through the mane.

My very first horse drawing does not compare with the work that I am doing now. I hope that I always improve. Of course I make mistakes, but I

have to move on; otherwise I'd still be stuck on that first drawing. I hope I never hit a ceiling where there is no longer any improvement. I never want to be complacent or bored.

People always ask me why I draw only horses. For thousands of years horses have been the inspiration and subjects of great works of art, and I can understand why when I am around them. They are the only artistic inspiration I have ever had. I will probably always draw horses and continue to use pencil as my medium because it gives me more control than anything else. Pencil allows me to reproduce in detail what I see and feel.

I love the life that my art has given me. I don't necessarily have to have my own ranch and my own horses, but I love being around them when I can. When a horse nuzzles me, I enjoy it and appreciate it. Those first horses were what got me started on the path I am on today. Maybe owning horses will be a possibility again, but for now I am happy to have the connection through art. Through my drawings I'm able to express my commitment to this magnificent creature.

# A DIFFERENT KIND OF OBSTACLE

## by *Georgina Bloomberg*

*There is something about jumping a horse
over a fence, something that makes you feel good.
Perhaps it's the risk, the gamble.
In any event it's a thing I need.*

—William Faulkner (1897–1962)

As a child, I was given my very first pony; the best present I could have ever dreamed of. I had been taking lessons at a local farm on an old and experienced pony, but I had always hoped for a pony to call my own. On the day that my parents surprised me with my new partner, Upsy Daisy, I thought that I was the luckiest person in the world.

For the next four years, Daisy was my heart and soul. With her kindness and experience, she taught me to love and trust horses. The first time I tumbled over her head, I was shocked that instead of running off, Daisy stopped and, with a look of concern and understanding in her eyes, waited for me to get back on and try again. I would never have guessed that such a large animal could have a heart that was even bigger. With her caring, I learned about the ways of horses: how to understand them; how to treat them; but most importantly, how to feel comfortable, appreciative, and trusting around them. When she passed away, I first felt as if I could not go on without her. As I grew older and moved on to other ponies and eventually horses, I began to see that I should not focus on my grief over her death, but rather focus on her life and what she gave and taught me. I could not let her lessons and the love of horses that she had instilled in me go to waste. I still miss her, but now when I think of Daisy, I can see how lucky I was to have had her to give me a strong foundation of love and trust around all horses.

One day, Daisy's lessons were put to the test. While schooling a horse with whom I was not very familiar over a water jump, a combination of horse and rider error caused me to have a fall. As a result of the hard ground and the impact with which I hit, I ended up with a fractured spine and significant loss of strength in one leg. After a number of days in the hospital, I was released in a body cast and given a cane for walking.

At first, the doctors had said that it would be months before I could take the cast off or start a rehabilitation program, and even longer before I could think of sitting on a horse. At this point, the longest I had ever gone without riding was a month, and thinking of just how difficult that time had been brought on a feeling of panic; I would have to wait possibly eight times as long before getting on a horse again. I felt as if the world would pass me by as I lay flat on my back, unable to stop it.

The next six months were a painful, frustrating, and depressing period of healing, doctors' visits, and physical therapy. What made this time worse was the realization I had one day while watching a video of a horse show: for the first time in my life, I was thoroughly terrified of getting back on a horse. As an experienced athlete, I was more than aware that there is always a certain amount of risk in everything that we do, but all of sudden I found that no matter how hard I tried, my fear of being hurt again had overpowered every rational thought. I had never been afraid before. I worried that my accident had damaged me more mentally than physically and that I would never be able to put that day behind me.

After a few months, I made the decision that I would get back in the saddle and slowly but surely try to become the brave and trusting rider I had once been. This was harder than I could have ever dreamed. I began slowly, simply walking and soon trotting. I found these simple acts to

be fun again, and soon I got the urge to move on to cantering. After a few weeks, the time had come for me to step up my comeback and begin jumping again. I knew that this would be the real test, and I found, as expected, that I could no longer trust the horse or myself. At every second I was expecting some mishap or drama. I no longer felt carefree or happy while on horseback because of my incessant fear and inability to trust. I loved being able to be around my horses again, but I still found myself wondering if I could continue to ride at all.

One night, I decided to take a look at my past to help me decide the fate of my future. I needed to recall my beginnings in the horse world and try to make sense of my feelings. As I flipped through pictures of myself as a child, I

began to remember all that my accident had made me forget. I love horses. I don't choose to ride, I have to ride. I need the feeling that you get from a gallop across a field or the rush of a winning round, but most of all, I need the loving bond that forms between horse and rider. I saw nothing but pure joy on my face in my old pictures, and everything that I loved finally came back to me. The fearlessness and trust in horses had not been born in me when I was a child, but rather instilled in me, first by Daisy and then by other ponies and horses down the road. Just like anything else, that took time, and that was perhaps all I needed to regain my balance in the horse world. I had let one accident endanger sixteen years of hard work and pure happiness by making me question my faith in what I loved. My mind was fixating on that one day, while it should be thinking about the rest of the fun and joy-filled years. I realized that I had to give myself time to trust again, as I had done when I was young, and that giving up was not an option. My love for horses was not something that I was willing to let myself throw away.

Now, almost six months after my return to the saddle, I feel that I am almost 100 percent back to my old self. I still have my moments of flashbacks from my fall, but I no longer feel insecure or mistrusting when riding. I know that it will just take time to fully recover from my fall, and now I know that I am doing the right thing by sticking to riding. I fully believe that fate chooses a path for everyone and life tests you to see if you can stick to it. I was born to ride, and now I see that one obstacle is not enough to take away my love for horses, which I hope to have for the rest of my life.

*After pondering Georgina's story, I turned to the* very first page of my Bible, the inside cover actually. I had scratched a note there some years earlier after hearing the sermon of a favorite pastor. I remembered that I had written something about fear, but I could not recall the quote. Inscribed on the inside cover are these words: "Persistence is the answer to fear." I have always found when working with fearful people and their horses that being willing to see an exercise through to completion is very important to the better understanding of their horses.

It seems that fear, our enemy, is brought to life when we lose understanding of a person, situation, activity, or even a horse. When we forget or realize who or what something is, we become fearful of it. I have experienced my own bouts with fear concerning horses, and those times are not among my favorite memories. How could I be afraid of something that I know so well?

I have been asked more than one hundred times how to overcome a recently developed fear of riding or of horses in general. I believe that the answer lies in understanding the horse or re-understanding the horse. More often than not, our fear of the horse comes when we are surprised by a turn of events. To be surprised, something must happen that we did not expect. I know that when I get to know a horse better through training, I am more apt to understand his actions and reactions, and I am less likely to be surprised.

There are thousands of books available that explore the question, "What is the horse?" There are no such books exploring the question, "Who is your horse in particular?" The only method that I know of to lessen the chance of surprise is to become better acquainted with your horse's responses. Perfecting ground exercises is the best way to become better acquainted with your horse's actions. Most students who are willing to focus on a prescribed set of exercises can work through their fears, but it requires persistent focus on the goal.

Sometimes I almost feel guilty prescribing such a practical solution for such an intangible type of problem, but the facts are that it is through groundwork that my own confidence in a horse and his reactions is bolstered.

lesley harrison
psa

# THE PATH FROM KILLER WHALES TO HORSES

## by *Shawna Karrasch*

*Nature has not placed us in an inferior rank to men, no more
than the females of other animals, where we see no distinction
of capacity, though I am persuaded if there was a common-
wealth of rational horses . . . it would be an established maxim
amongst them that a mare could not be taught to pace.*

—Mary Wortley Montagu (1689–1762),
Letter to her daughter

# There is something

magical about women and horses. The two seem to go hand in hand, or more appropriately hand in hoof. This starts early. Girls go from caring for their dolls to pining for a horse. For many girls, this dream doesn't become a reality. Many girls who are fortunate enough to have a horse have to relinquish him at some point as a thing of youth. As women, most of them maintain their warm memories of horses. Many women whom I have spoken to who have always wanted a horse now have the resources to achieve their dream. Their horses are passions they hold dear. They harbor, protect, and defend them, whether their charges are gentle or ornery. They speak of their horses with great pride.

My path to horses, however, was not the usual one. My current passion for horses actually started with marine mammals. That's right, killer whales, dolphins, sea lions, walruses, and otters. I trained animals at Sea World using reward, or positive, reinforcement for nearly ten years. I then took the reward reinforcement training to horses. I now educate people about horse behavior. I help them work with a better understanding of their horses.

Let's get back to the beginning of my experience with horses, the path that led to my current admiration. I had a somewhat troubled childhood. From a very young age I found that not all people could be trusted. Animals, I decided as a child, were the most honest beings on the planet. This is when my early trust and intense interest in animals developed. In addition to household pets, I was exposed to farm animals. My grandfather had a farm, where my father would take me to visit as far back as I can remember. Of course there were horses on the farm; these old guys were as broke as they get. They would not do

anything except when told, and even then it sometimes took considerable persuasion. As soon as I was old enough to become cognizant of their behavior, I realized that they didn't seem to enjoy our company. I felt better just leaving them alone, and so I did.

While working at Sea World twenty-five years later, I learned more about animal behavior. It dawned on me why our horses behaved as they did. Traditionally, we have used removal reinforcement to train horses: we squeeze our legs, and when the horse starts walking, we remove the pressure. Horses trained this way performed well enough, but not necessarily with enthusiasm. This is nothing like the reward reinforcement we use at Sea World. Considering the way most horses have been trained, I didn't understand why horses do anything for us at all. I realized that I could change

horses' attitudes, that I could alter the way they perceive people. My interest in horse training escalated until one day, at the age of thirty-two, I took my first riding lesson. I was hooked. I was an adult who was like every ten-year-old girl in the country. I was horse crazy!

I wanted to help people better understand, communicate with, and motivate their horses. Ultimately I knew this would help horses have a better quality of life and enjoy their jobs, whatever those might be. This gets to the crux of why I find horses so endearing, in fact even good for my soul. Early on, I made a decision that I did not want to be a part of anyone's life, be it human or animal, unless I added something to his or her life, making it better in some way. I know I'm not the only one who feels this way. I see it in female horse owners all the time. Their faces light up when they talk about their horses, share their stories. Some become concerned or worried about an issue their horse is having. They have the kind of look a mother has when her child

or someone else she loves needs help. She feels it's her job to make it better.

There's something about a horse—majestic, free, and proud—that reaches almost all of us. He stands before us full of grace and purity. This is something women recognize and to which they respond. I have witnessed women taking on the worst cases, sometimes even dangerous horses. Bear in mind, these women are not experienced horse trainers, but instead women who are reacting from their hearts. When they see a horse who is truly misunderstood, they feel they can make him better given the right amount of compassion and patience. This touches me over and over again. I relate to these women: the desire to improve this magnificent animal's life, to add something good, to make a difference. This has become my mission in life, my reinforcement. When I see a woman's face light up when she's working in *simpatico* with her horse, well, I just couldn't have a better day. Yes, there is something magical about women and horses.

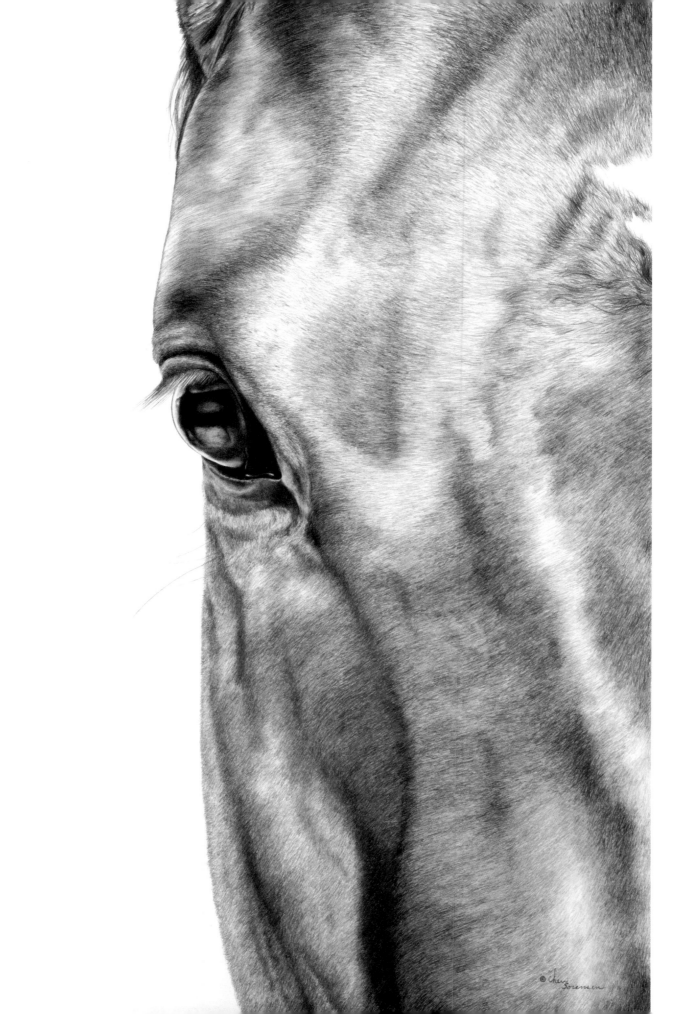

# FINDING YOUR PASSION

*by Cheri Sorensen*

*For want of a naile the shoe is lost,*
*for want of a shoe the horse is lost,*
*for want of a horse the rider is lost.*

—George Herbert (1593–1633),
*Jacula Prudentum*

*When I look* back on my childhood, I see a little girl drawing for hours at the dining room table. This became my make-believe studio and a quiet place to draw. As with many girls my age, horses were my passion. I would lose myself in the task of creating pictures for my friends and myself. Many of my friends still have those pictures.

As a fourth grader, I was one of the founding members of an "elite" group of girls called the Horse Club. In our minds we were a highly sophisticated and knowledgeable group of future equestrians. Recess was our official meeting time, when we had in-depth discussions about the names of our horses, which none of us had, and how well we would be able to jump and ride. I wanted to be a jockey, feeling it would be a great way to spend time around horses when I became an adult.

My incessant requests for a horse no doubt drove my parents crazy. I'm sure they dreaded getting my Christmas and birthday lists. They would roll their eyes at the first choice on each list. They did, however, notice a talent for drawing in their tomboy daughter, which they believed might benefit from professional lessons. They also let me work as a trail guide at a local riding stable to help fulfill that strange desire in me they didn't fully understand.

Studying and drawing still-life and human portraits, with a Hungarian instructor, was not my first choice of subjects, especially at the age of fourteen. But I would go home after class and draw horses to hang on my walls or give to my friends. I stuck with the lessons for two or three years, though, and was able to learn quite a bit about lighting and cast shadows.

At the age of fifteen, I painted a quarter horse on my bedroom wall (it is still there). The walls were pink at that time, and the horse was two feet tall and three feet wide. He sported a western saddle with a colorful blanket. A welcoming barn was later added in the background. I had not asked permission from my parents to do the painting; in other words, I had not been given "creative license." Surprise was their first reaction at finding me redecorating the walls. Then to my relief, they looked forward to seeing the finished product. They laugh about that today. The room has since been repainted, but not before my dad built a huge frame to surround the painting. Today, the walls are an antique white while the painting and the pink wall still shine from inside the frame. It is a fun memory, but what I didn't realize then is that this was really just the beginning for me.

I became a full-time artist in the early '90s, attending various wildlife banquets, displaying and

selling my work at art shows. Commission work was a large part of my business, composed of everything from dogs and cats to hunting scenes. I was creating, yes, but I was creating what I thought was necessary for me to be able to make it as a full-time artist. Basically, I had strayed from my true artistic passion.

After realizing what a true "horse nut" he had married, my husband decided it was time to make my dream of owning a horse come true. Max, an American paint, was a little six-month-old when we first met. When I think back to that day now, I believe we actually chose each other. Max was one of four babies my husband and I looked at that day. They were all a bit skittish and shy, all but one little guy who reached as far as he could over the fence to go nose-to-nose with me, wanting to see what we were all about.

The inspirations for equestrian drawings and paintings began whirling through my head as Max and I began our journey of becoming partners and trusting each other. There were a few warmbloods in the barn where I boarded Max, and I soon found that for a mere pocketful of carrots, they were extremely photogenic. It was an awesome feeling standing in the middle of three horses ranging between 17 and 18.2 hands, all interested in the crunchy treats I carried in my pocket. This created an opportunity for up close and personal photo shoots. So after almost twenty years, I once again began to draw my passion. I printed a few of the drawings and decided to try selling them at our Iowa Horse Fair. I'm not sure words can express the feeling I got from seeing people truly moved by a piece of artwork created from my own heart and hand.

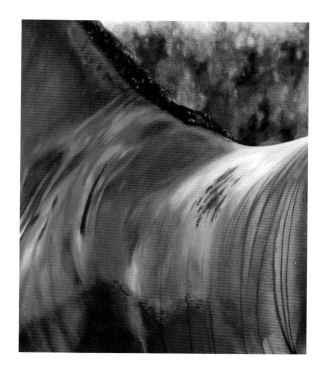

My husband joined me full time just a few years ago, and we now travel the country coast to coast, showing my work at major equestrian events and shows. I occasionally give drawing lessons in my hometown and do seminars while at some shows. The ideas for new drawings are now so numerous that I find the only difficult part is trying to keep up with them.

The time I spend with Max is my relaxation. All the stress of booking shows or filling orders goes right out the barn door when I can bury my face in his mane and breathe in his earthy sweet scent. The connection we have today is so much like those I hear about every day from other horse lovers as they wander through my booth during shows.

Rediscovering my passion for horses and having the opportunity to share it with others is a little girl's dream come true. Finding and staying true to your passion truly are words to live by.

# THE HORSE: MY TEACHER, MY FRIEND

## by Debbie Dolan-Sweeney

*No one can teach riding
so well as a horse.*

—C. S. Lewis (1898–1963),
*The Horse and His Boy*

*When I reflect* on my lifetime involvement with horses, I think of timeless beauty. My experiences as a small child feeding carrots to horses through a fence at a nearby farm are just as unique and special for me as the thrilling moments of grand prix show jumping. Why is that? How is that? The answer lies in the changing yet timeless relationships forged with horses. The bonds formed with horses go beyond snapshot moments in time. As wonderful as these moments are, it is the depth of joy and warmth that these special animals give you everyday. No two horses are the same, and no two moments are the same. As a whole they create an internal strength, courage, and character to can take with you over a lifetime.

Starting from a very young age when a career with horses was still a twinkle of a dream, I began bonding with horses. Esquire and Crimson Imp were two ponies I shared with my sister. We split everything from chores to riding. We even chose who could brush the right or left side of the pony and who got to braid a mane or a tail. We lived and breathed these animals. Although their physical talents were small compared with those of grand prix mounts of future years, their part in the development of my passion and love for horses was huge. Next came Ruby Tuesday. She was my magical stepping-stone horse. She was very small, but her heart of gold brought me from schooling shows to advanced equitation competitions. She gave me the courage to find wings, to believe that anything was possible.

I was seventeen. I knew I had learned a lifetime of lessons from horses already. It was time to go to college, forget horses, and start a new stage in life. So went the plan in my head but not in my heart. It took less than two weeks to discover this plan was not for me. There must be some way to continue my education in horses as well as follow my academic aspirations. Was it possible to complete college and continue riding at a level higher then I ever thought possible? The answer was yes if I committed to three key principles: desire, determination, and discipline. Unaware at the time, I was about to enter into a stage in my career that would be the foundation for all that was to come.

I remember many nights in airport terminals writing papers and studying for exams. Oftentimes I would get back to my dorm room in early morning with classes beginning in just a few short hours. My weekdays were booked solid to allow for weekend competitions. My school friends would talk about the fun campus weekends, but I never

felt that I was missing out. My relationship with horses was strong and unwavering. I think some important people in my life worried this straight-line, almost tunnel-vision approach would not allow me to see other opportunities available to me. It was a valid concern, but what neither they nor I understood completely at the time was how much this lifestyle would help me with other endeavors further down the road.

So as college progressed, my relationship with incredible animals continued. Country was my buddy. He was an American Thoroughbred, fast as lightening. This horse truly believed he should live in the house and eat at the family dining table. His can-do attitude led us to many national and international victories. His spirit of kindness and happiness remains with me always.

At about the same time, I partnered up with a horse called Albany. Albany was to be my first grand prix horse. First, however, he would give my whole family a thrill by winning an Olympic gold medal with my coach at the time, Leslie Burr. This horse never had a negative thought. Sweet and gentle, he took care of me wherever we went. His list of accomplishments and trophies is large, but not close to the size of his heart.

Christmas of 1995 was a very special day. Under the tree was a large red box seemingly empty. Under the layers of tissue was a beautiful drawing done by my mother of a black stallion. An unimaginable Christmas gift, VIP was a big challenge. In the beginning I felt overwhelmed. How could I relate to this powerfully strong animal? I've always believed my physical abilities with horses were not as strong as my mental abilities. I absolutely had to form a one-to-one unique relationship with a horse before any competi-

tion success could occur. This made me a poor "catch rider," but the rewards were still plentiful, maybe even better. VIP showed me how time, patience, and understanding can lead to big dreams. I'm still amazed at how even the most unlikely of horse-rider combinations can work if you can create an understanding. VIP was the perfect example of this.

Quantum Leap was a small horse with a big attitude. He tested me thoroughly before a relationship really began to form. On quick outside appearance, this looked to be a good match. His size and style were perfect for me. However, outside looks do not always match inside feelings. We started with a lot of doubts about each other. Popular opinion was that Quantum did not have enough ability. This was the first time I had to do the convincing. I had to believe and then instill confidence in him. Sometimes early on he would act up, maybe peak or dodge a water jump in his snarky way. It was as if he were trying to show off his dominance to hide his nerves. I could feel this in him and learned how to turn that negative energy into positive energy. There was no stopping us after that. We thrived off each other. We gave each other confidence on competition day.

Itziweeni was my soul mate, my glove fit. We formed a bond quickly. She always had a never-look-back attitude. Although only 15.2 hands, she was convinced there was no horse bigger or better then she. I first saw she four years before we would actually become partners. It must have been destiny, because our paths kept crossing, and eventually we became a team. She started out as a nice speed horse, but with time together and special bonding, she became the 1997 AHSA Open Jumper Horse of the Year; quite an accomplishment for a horse standing barely 15.2 hands. Itzi remains the queen of the barn to this day.

All of these horses were unique. All taught me separate but enduring lessons on how to live my own life. I don't measure the success of my career in ribbons and trophies. My career has been and continues to be highlighted by special bonds with unique animals who teach lessons of everyday life.

I recently went back to school to pursue a master's degree in nutrition. It took me three years to complete all the courses through online education. This meant again I was using the principles desire, determination, and discipline to accomplish my goals. I can remember studying organic chemistry in the farm apartment with my three-month-old daughter, Claire, at my side. I had made up my mind that I wanted to continue school, continue with horses, and be the best mom I possibly could. It may have seemed like a lot to undertake at once, but I was fully prepared. Horses had again given me the strength to achieve such a task.

My greatest achievements by far, though, are my children. Claire is now five and Connor is three. Our triplets, Helen, Sean, and Corinne, are one-year old. From the very beginning, I knew the importance of patience and understanding. Loving them came naturally. It is not something to be learned. Dealing with toddlers, though, is a new experience. People often ask us how we do it with five children under five years old. You have to be calm, understanding, and patient, all the while helping them to learn and accept their emotions. Here I had a big pool of experience to use.

Special relationships and bonds with horses do not necessarily happen overnight. Sometimes you feel that magic connection immediately.

Other times it takes a lot of work with patience and understanding at the center of every lesson. Feeling their emotions and knowing how and when to react is extremely important. I now see my life and relationship with horses as a beautiful gift that helps me with my greatest challenge—raising my children.

Competition will always be in my blood. Horses, though, have given me more than that. They have shown me what true passion is. They have given me courage to try anything I want. They fill a part of my soul with a warmth that some people never experience. I can pursue anything in my life at any time as long as I stay true to the lessons and principles I originally learned with horses. These experiences are my real memories and the ones I want to teach and share with my children.

*While reading Debbie's essay and her description of* her horses, I thought for a moment about all of the equine friends I have had over the years. I would like to share a few of the most memorable with you.

Ben, quarter horse, age twenty-something: In the fall of 2001, I attended a camp horse sale at the infamous New Holland Auction. It is only infamous, by the way, due to rumors and circumstance. It is not much different from any other auction that I have been to. Ben is the only horse I have ever bought based on his training. I was immediately impressed as he trotted past me in the auction alley. He was an older quarter horse, 200–250 lbs, underweight, dehydrated, had rain rot, yet he responded to the lightest of cues from his rider. He was visibly malnourished, but he did not hesitate to perform one single maneuver. Walk, trot, canter, sliding stop, side-pass, roll back—someone had spent a long time teaching this horse to go lightly. SOLD! One hundred and twenty-five dollars later, Ben was in my trailer, headed home to be loved to health by my daughter. After winning forty or fifty ribbons at the local barrel races, Ben let me know that he might be getting a little old for can chasing. Ben now lives near Green Cove Springs, Florida, and teaches youngsters how to do the barrel pattern.

Rio, Tennessee walking horse, age fourteen: A Mennonite friend of mine told me about a horse named Tommy who was for sale at his barn. He told me that someone had tried to turn him into a team horse and had messed up his gait. Sure enough, when I rode him he really did not know how to put one foot in front of another. In the meadow he was fine, but get on his back and you had scrambled legs underneath you. I bought him for a few hundred dollars and took him home. After a little diagnosis, Rio (his new name) told us that it was the bit and thinking about the bit that had messed up his ability to gait. I put a rope halter on Rio, attached some reins, and down the lane we went, as

*smooth as any Tennessee walker ever gaited. Since then, I have developed the PonyBoy Bitless, a side-pull-type hackamore made of rope halter material. Thousands of horses have Rio to thank for the more comfortable bridle that their owners now use. Rio lives outside of Saint Augustine, Florida.*

*Copy (Patchy's Hot Copy), Appaloosa, age twenty-eight: Copy is a gem. He currently lives at Mill Creek Farms, a retirement home for horses. He is blind and lives in a forty-acre pasture with seven other elderly, blind, Appaloosas. This is the horse who made a horsewoman out of my daughter. There are very few horses with a history like Copy's. He is one of the last foals from a very important foundation mare to the Appaloosa breed. He spent most of his life teaching girls to ride at two prominent riding schools. Copy appeared in two reference books,* The Ultimate Horse *and* The Complete Horse Encyclopedia. *He lived at the Kentucky Horse Park for four to five years and participated in its daily Parade of Breeds. And he did something that even he doesn't know about.*

*I was hired as a consultant for the movie* Spirit *several years ago. After speaking to the animators for a few hours, I was given a tour of DreamWorks Studios in Burbank. As I passed one of the animator's offices, I noticed a poster-size picture of an Appaloosa on his wall. I said to the animator, "That's Copy on your wall." He said, "No, it's an original." "No," I said, "That is my daughter's horse Copy." Although there is a real buckskin mustang named Spirit who was used as a subject for the animator, he was not buff enough. So Copy, a twenty-something Appaloosa, was used as a conformational model for the animators. Copy would get a kick out of that story.*

*If you are ever in Alachua, Florida, stop by Mill Creek. There are more than one hundred retired horses there who can always use a little love.*

SylRBy

# KEEPING THE FLAME OF CLASSICISM ALIGHT

*by Sylvia Loch*

*The horse will leap over trenches,*
*will jump out of them, will do anything else,*
*provided one grants him praise*
*and respite after his accomplishment.*

—Xenophon (430–355 BC)

# In celebrating my

passion for horses and the art of equitation, I know that had it not been for two men in my life, things might have been very different. First, my father: Alexander Gordon Beauchamp Cameron was a man whom I can only describe as a natural creator. He could turn his hand to anything: playing the fiddle; sketching by a lonely loch; mixing his oil paints as he worked a huge studio portrait; staining glass for a cathedral window; dabbling with watercolor; telling marvelous stories; restoring a derelict house; building a conservatory, an apiary, a rabbit hutch, a children's trapeze; tending bees—this man also found time to build stables for an adoring daughter, even when time and money were tight. Daddy to me, Sandy to his friends, I still miss him. With a twinkle in his eye and music in his step, his able, generous hands could make miracles happen.

My father never had the opportunity to ride as I did. His father had been a cavalryman. Before they ran out of money, my grandparents filled their Edinburgh house with nineteenth-century sporting prints by J. F. Herring, which if sold at auction today would have bought real racehorses! But in his innate, sensitive way, Daddy knew about horses, and he knew about being quiet with them; I watched as they gravitated toward him. And it was the same with all animals. So even at a very young age, I saw my father was special. Not only did he introduce me to horses, but he also opened my eyes to beauty and a respect for the natural world around us. I believe it is that balance of beauty and respect that has set me on my chosen path.

Then there was my husband, Lord Henry, who left me a widow at the age of thirty-seven, with twenty-two horses and a baby daughter. An irrever-

ent, dyslectic, alcoholic, colorful, peer of the realm, former cavalry instructor, and wonderful rider of horses, Henry was the one who introduced me to the Lusitanos and the Andalusians, the great riding academies of Europe, and the classical way of riding.

The first time I saw Henry ride, he looked like a statue, but the horse was all liquid movement. And of all the riders I have ever watched, Henry really knew how to balance a horse; even nonhorse people could see that! With the lightest of hands on the rein and no visible effort, and with a smile on his lips, Henry could bring a big, fiery stallion back on his hocks just by sitting tall and squaring his shoulders.

These two men played a huge part in my life, not only enriching me through love, but also leaving a legacy of awe, an awe that never fails to grip

when I see a horse in a field, touch a horse in a stable, or feel a horse under me. Although they have long since gone, the influence of these men and their regard for the classical arts has lived on. The image of Henry in a slow, collected canter has taught me lightness and has shown me that less is more. My father's love of beauty, our visits to the great galleries, his simple lessons on perspective and balance have led me on a constant quest for harmony. Riding should look, as well as feel, beautiful.

I guess it would be smug to say that we women understand horses better than men do. I do, however, think we have a gift for explaining things better, particularly our feelings toward horses. I also think we may need horses more; for many women, horses can be a substitute for a job, a partner, a child—who knows? And certainly, horses enable us to express ourselves more freely. Added to that, there is no doubt that our maternal instincts can come unashamedly to the fore in our relationships with horses. But in countries where men still dominate the equestrian disciplines, as in Portugal and Spain and the Americas with mounted bullfighting and herding, there are still some amazing natural horsewomen. The more they depend on the horse for their lives, the greater the partnership, the more the respect.

So what motivates me with my horses? There was a time when I was quite enthused with competition, and certainly a modicum of success at dressage and breed shows brought a certain pleasure. Now, that has changed. I no longer hanker after these things. And I don't really want to teach others whose only obsession is to win because too many will keep their secrets to themselves; then who will pass on the knowledge? No, it's the future that disturbs and motivates me all at the same time. People are in too great a hurry today: in their haste for medals, most are bypassing the old ways. Horses are being rushed and in some cases are cast away, almost like a fashion accessory, if they are not up to scratch. Who is there to speak up for them?

As I've become older, I've felt a deep yearning to give back to the horse something of what has been given to us—gifts such as generosity and patience and the time and freedom to soar! So when a horse comes before me in a riding arena, immediately I am caught up in it all; it's no longer just another lesson. I am there to give back and to help, and I want the rider to help her horse, too. This can be hard because often I immediately see that the horse and the rider are out of balance and out of tune, so there is a lot of work to be done. Empathetic riders will know this, which is why these people come to me.

It may sound like nonsense, but everything inside me cringes when a horse is out of balance— the worse the case, the more I respond to it. Yes, nowadays I actually seem to feel what I am seeing and I guess this is a gift, but it is also a responsibility. Whether it comes from God or from the horses themselves, I am not sure; I only know it happens and that the horse is expectant. So when I feel/see the horse as a beast of burden, out of sync, and with his life and movements a drudgery, I need to find the words to help him. As he eyes me sideways across the arena, a *cri de coeur* in those liquid depths, I know he wants to be balanced, empowered, and made beautiful again. Most of all, he needs to be comfortable and at one with his rider. And that is where I come in.

There are so many things to consider even before we work on position: the horse's conformation, his muscling or lack of it, his saddle, the rider's weight. These can be so radically wrong for that horse. Sometimes I meet horses with eyes that don't speak, who have simply given up: too much pain over too many years has taken away their desire to be helped. It is probably too late for them. But for most, I can always make changes for the better. Using imagery can help enormously, and I believe being female makes it easier for me to give people at least a sense of the right feelings, to help their techniques help their horses. And miraculously, in turn, the horses blossom under our love, seeming to know when our intentions are pure.

We women are not afraid to talk about feelings—whether it's mental or physical. With the latter, all the biomechanical things that we have to do with our bodies, particularly when giving birth, are ever-present in our minds. In today's liberated society, we are not afraid to talk about physical feeling: pelvic floor tone, thigh stretches, bosom lifts (natural of course!), and so on. When I wrote *The Classical Seat*, I had no idea how revolutionary my readers would find it. I had simply tried to describe what I felt on horseback when I first went to Portugal and sat on those highly tuned Lusitano horses. I knew that almost everything I learned to do with them was down to nuances of feeling. Indeed, my only condemnation of some of the maestros' teachings was that they rarely described how it felt—almost never in their books. Even my late husband seemed at a loss for words if a student asked him exactly how it felt. He'd look at the student a little sideways, describe the aids by the book, and then add, "Well, you know, you just do it!" While he

exercised his own particular magic, I was fast developing a language by which a rider's sense of feeling could develop. I'd talk about swelling up and growing proud like those grand old military commanders one sees in ancient equestrian portraits. For passage I would say, "Grow tall and raise your center of gravity and reach for the sky!" To sit the trot I'd say, "Let go with the pelvic floor and soften your seat muscles"; or to keep the stirrups I'd say, "Open your hips and throw your lower leg away!" I noticed my female riders really identified with all this, and even the men seemed to find it helpful.

But I guess none of this practical stuff would work without the background of theory. My long apprenticeship in Portugal, the research, the watching, the interviews, the great riders, the classic books, the thinking, and the scholarship—all this accumulated knowledge has left me with something to offer. Lucky enough to step onto Portuguese soil at the end of an era, prerevolution, pre–European Commission, people like me had stumbled upon something unique. Here was a culture, once the prerogative of the courts and the elite cavalry schools, that was rapidly fading from today's world of sport riding before our very eyes. If we did not act soon, the art might be lost forever. Surely it was up to us to keep alive these practices and techniques, sharing them with others and demonstrating them in our own riding and in our own horses. In France, I found other people who felt the same, a few in Denmark, Sweden, others scattered overseas. We all needed to work together, to keep alive the spirit of classicism. Only then can that fine golden thread, the knowledge, remain intact.

And here again, I believe women have helped and will continue to do so. We can exercise our

imagination and passion and encourage others to follow this route. We can talk about how it feels to be a horse and point out at the basic level how illogical and damaging it is to thump about on a horse's back and kick his sides. At a higher level, we need to keep in mind young joints and the damage invoked by tight nosebands and artificial contraptions that force a horse's neck into a position that God never gave him. We can remind people of the horse's beauty. We can point out that wonderful engineering of his muscles and joints and the way his neck rises naturally out of high withers into a recreation of a Velasquez canvas.

As women, we should not be afraid to bare our souls a little. We can speak of how we marvel at the way in which this great creature is willing to give and bend his whole powerful body and his natural pride to our will. We can speak of the gift he makes to us when he shows that he is willing to submit to us. Once people are reminded of how mind blowing it all can be, attitudes change.

And so, there is power as I write. I often wonder whence it comes. There are passages in my books that I scarcely remember writing, although I know I did it. But of one thing I'm certain: the more I want to share the knowledge, the more knowledge comes. Riding makes me more creative, the wholesomeness and rhythm of the horse's body stirs my soul.

There was a time when I tried to take a break from teaching. I tried to write children's stories and find an easier life. Gradually I became aware that I was laboring down the wrong track; I was meant to be writing about what my horses taught me, continuing to teach me, not messing about with jolly tales that had all been told too many times before.

Maybe it helped that I am a woman and recognized this fairly early in my career. Maybe a man would have stuck to Plan A, who knows? All I know is that the moment I sat down to write about riding, everything changed. In fact, my life took off as each horse, each student yielded new knowledge. Understanding, natural respect, imagination, and awe are my foundations.

As an artist's daughter, I know that balance is everything: balance in nature, balance in our lives, balance in the horse. And I know that people and horses need to be helped. Isn't that what the classical ethos is all about: purity of line, economy of movement, just a small adjustment here, a brushstroke there? With God's help, and the help of all those people who feel the same, we can change the whole picture.

# A PART OF THE HERD

*by Julie Goodnight*

*Some of my best leading men
have been dogs and horses.*

—Elizabeth Taylor,
American actress

# My humble begin-

nings with horses have enlightened me not only to the ways and wiles of horses, but also to how it is that women are so inextricably intertwined with them, for better or for worse, and why horses are so powerfully attractive to women.

Growing up on a small horse farm in central Florida, I received my first informal lessons in horse behavior began at an early age. I was fortunate to have had the opportunity to develop and explore my passion for horses, which was passed on to me from my father. Being one of four siblings who all had the same opportunities and exposures, I was the only one in my family who was caught in the web. To say I had an interest in horses is a gross understatement, for if I had been able to transform myself into a horse, I would have gone to live with the herd in a heartbeat.

As an introverted child, my days were spent hiding out in the pastures with the horses. Although I was shy and quiet in my youth, I came to life with horses. Some of my fondest childhood memories are of the hours and days spent in my fort in the huge tree out in the pasture. My sanctuary also provided a refuge to our horses from the hot Florida sun, and we spent a lot of quality time there, hidden in the shade of the huge oak. While my parents worried that I did not have many friends, I found camaraderie with the herd. And while my parents were concerned that I never seemed to talk much, the dialogue with my herd mates was never ending. My infatuation turned to a lifetime passion.

It wasn't until I was a young adult that I began to question where my connection to horses came from and how I had gained the ability to understand horses so well. How was it that I knew things about horses that no one had ever taught me? Was it genetic memory? Was I born with some sort of sixth sense or mystical ability that allowed me to communicate with horses in a way others couldn't grasp?

I remember a big brown Thoroughbred that belonged to a timid middle-aged rider. They were a bad match and their relationship was troubled, to say the least. Both horse and rider were anxious and struggling to communicate. I was drawn into this tumultuous relationship in an effort to help both of them. At the age of fourteen, I was a competent rider. I knew how to jump big fences and I could ride just about anything with four legs. But no one had ever taught me much about horse behavior or how to train a horse. As I worked with the brown horse, I somehow managed to connect with him, find the source of the horse's anxiety, and help both horse and rider find confidence in each other. Using

my intuition, I was able to provide the horse with an understanding of what was expected of him and give the owner a sense of how to relate to the horse.

Gradually, I came to realize that my understanding of horses had come from the horses themselves and my days spent in the company of the herd under the big oak tree. By immersing myself in their lives, I had learned their rules and the communicative gestures and various behaviors of the individuals. Armed with this invaluable but subconscious understanding, I began my career with horses and started on the infinite path toward greater insight.

Having spent the past twenty-five years as a female horse trainer in a traditionally male industry, I've thought a great deal about how women and men differ in their approaches to horses. I have been teaching people about horses for most of my life, and I know that there are clear differences between the genders. So what is it about women and horses that can account for the unique bond between the two?

For the most part, women possess qualities that enhance our relationship with horses; but some of these traits can get in our way. In general, women are much more intuitive than men and are more in tune to emotions. Since horses are largely nonverbal communicators and highly emotional animals, I think women have a leg up on men when it comes to being able to understand the horse and connect with and understand his emotions. Not only can women sense the emotionality in others, but we also tend to take on those emotions more easily, thus making us more empathetic.

Women are nurturers by nature. We are programmed to take care of our "herd." We are more inclined to function in family groups and watch out for the greater good of the group. Like the boss mare in the horse herd, we seek food and shelter, provide discipline and structure, and guard against threats to the safety of those in our care. In essence, we have a tendency to be herd-bound ourselves.

On a deeper level, I believe women can connect with horses from a shared understanding of what it is like to be a prey animal. Although humans are considered to be predators and in fact have been the number one predator of horses for more than 150,000 years, women are more accustomed to being prey than being predator. Throughout history, there have been women who have been oppressed and victimized by individual males who are physically stronger by nature. Throughout history, society has oppressed women in many ways. Both women and horses understand what it means to be vulnerable, and I think that as a result, both horses and women are connected deep within as strong, spirited animals with true vulnerabilities that lie just below the surface. As women, we know what it is like to have our rights infringed upon. We know what it is like to fear for our own safety and survival. In some cases, we understand what it is like to be captive and powerless to determine our own fates.

I spent my college years working at a racetrack. I loved the riding; I loved the excitement of busting out of the starting gate and running like the wind. I loved the challenge of riding young, vigorous horses and staying with them through their transition from gangly colts to mature and resolute athletes. I loved the power that I felt riding racehorses. Yet walking through the back barns at the track, I would cower from the catcalls and the harassment emanating from the seedy track workers. As a rider, I felt strong and empowered. As a woman, I felt vulnerable and frightened.

When a horse feels frightened and trapped, he sometimes forgets that he is strong and powerful and capable of defending himself because his nature is to run, not to confront. Sometimes a horse quietly accepts his fate and endures endless abuse, forgetting he has the power to fight back. At the track, I could handle the powerful and exuberant horses, but one pathetic and meaningless man could make me run for cover.

Just as men tend to approach life with bravado, women tend to approach life with cunning and finesse. I believe this accounts for why horses relate differently to men and women, for better or for worse. Whether it is a fact of biology or society, men generally are stronger and more confident than women and therefore tend to approach horses more from the perspective of muscling the horse or "conquering the savage beast." While women, with a keener sense of survival, an understanding of vulnerability, and knowing that our brute force will not count for much against a thousand-pound animal, tend to approach horses with greater finesse and thoughtfulness.

I believe it is this very difference that accounts for why we hear that horses are afraid of men. I do not think that horses can actually distinguish between the genders of humans, but they do react to the body language, attitudes, and intentions of men, who are generally more imposing and intimidating in their demeanors than women are. It has been my observation that horses who are supposedly afraid of men are not frightened by men who are quiet, calm, and humble in their approaches to horses. In other words, horses are not frightened by men "in touch with their feminine sides."

Although women seem to connect with horses through a shared sense of vulnerability, this sense of vulnerability can also manifest in a lack of confidence, which may interfere with a satisfactory relationship between the two. As men tend to approach horses with confidence and an air of leadership, women often approach horses with uncertainty and insecurity. Horses are quick to perceive the absence of leadership and may take advantage of a woman more quickly than they would a man.

The structure of the horse herd is a linear hierarchy, which means that each and every individual in the herd is either dominant over or subordinate to each and every other individual. In essence, you and your horse form a herd of two. You are either dominant or subordinate; you are either the leader or the follower. To earn respect and become the leader of the herd, a horse must control the resources of the herd, such as food and water, and control the space and actions of the subordinates. I have found that women often have difficulty stepping into the leadership role in their herds of two. Women are nurturers, not aggressors; therefore it is easy for us to fall into the subordinate role. We may be quick to let horses push us around and control our space, which only serves to convince the horse that he is, in fact, the alpha individual in the herd of two.

So while women have much strength that allows us to connect with horses on a deeper level, sometimes these strengths can become our greatest weaknesses. We are not as accustomed to defending our space and asking for what we want. We are more accustomed to giving of ourselves to others.

One of the best lessons women can learn and apply to our relationships with horses is to remember that we share much with them, and although we can relate to them naturally, our natural behaviors are potentially counterproductive

to capable management of our horses. In other words, how we feel—our emotions and intuitions—are positives; but how we react—whether we are confident and direct, or less assertive and indirect—can be negatives. If we can learn to use our senses and feelings to understand and bond with our horses, and if we can also learn to act directly and confidently, we will develop extraordinary bonds with our horses.

I have learned much from my lifetime spent with horses, and horses will continue to be my teachers throughout the rest of my life. I have learned to be honest, forthright, and clear in my communications with others. I have learned to follow through with my requests, an assertiveness that does not come naturally to women who are used to giving rather than taking. I have learned to feel confident and act like the leader, even when deep down inside I may not really feel that way. Sometimes, I just have to fake it.

Above all else, horses have taught me to be patient. I have learned to be persistent, to hold my ground and wait, and to let the horse come to me. There is no greater satisfaction than to develop a relationship with a horse that is based on trust and confidence. Perhaps the greatest lesson in patience is knowing that I will continue to learn about horses throughout the rest of my life. The tree fort of my childhood has given way to my kitchen table, where I sip coffee in the early morning hours and study the herd right outside my window. And no matter how hard I try and no matter how long I work at it, there will always be another lesson to be learned from a horse.

# HORSE-WOMAN

### by Lola Michelin

*A woman never looks better
than on horseback.*

—Jane Austen (1689–1762),
*The Watsons*

*I believe that* women are like horses because we are both so easy to get to know yet we both take a lifetime to comprehend.

Most of the women I know are horsewomen. Women who have their nails done regularly or choose of their own volition to wear skirts are fairly foreign to me. Most of the women I know prefer jeans and would rather drive a pickup than a sports car. And while I may not be able to parallel park, I can back up a truck to a trailer hitch with frightening accuracy.

I am among the group of people who think that horsewomen and horsemen are more similar than they are different. In a world where men and women are said to come from different planets, at least horsemen and horsewomen have a common language. In general, horse people are like horses to me—I can't seem to get enough of them.

Being a woman myself, I have limited insight into the relationship between horses and men. I have known several exceptional horsemen from whom I have learned a great deal about horses (and very little about men). In my experience, men certainly have proven to be handy to have around, and they do seem to know all the best (or worst) jokes. They do lack the mystery, however, that draws me to horses and to the women who love them.

Like most of the horsewomen I know, I simply cannot imagine life without horses, nor can I ever remember a time when horses were not a part of my life. I didn't have the good fortune of being born into horses, yet they were an ever-present force. As a child, my room was wallpapered with posters of Secretariat, Wing Commander, and the Black Stallion. Breyer models grazed across the top of my dresser and bedded down in my strewn clothes. As soon as I could read, I checked out every horse book our town library had and started scouring the classifieds, memorizing the ads for horses looking for "good homes only," a habit I carry around to this day. My girlhood friends and I pranced around our backyards, neighing wildly, herding and roping any dog or cat too slow to escape us. On rainy days, we imagined the names of all the horses we would have one day, drew plans for their shed rows, and chose the colors of our silks and tack trunks. On weekends, I would ride my cousin's little bay pony, appropriately named Nipper, grinning as I trotted in endless circles.

I prayed for each summer to arrive, when my parents would take me to a horse camp in Ontario. Those blissful days I spent steeped in the rich smells of Canadian timothy and oiled leather. Perhaps that was when I first recognized the deep connection between women and horses. That camp was a pleasure paradise for a bunch of horse-crazy girls. We spent every breathing moment with the horses. We shared the cool water pooling out of the hose with them, feeling the prickly whiskers against our cheeks. We wore bracelets around our ankles and wrists that were braided from the tail hairs of our favorite horses, plucked carefully from the brushes and combs. We swam in the shallow pond with the ponies, clambering onto their backs in the deep water and twisting our fingers in their coarse manes as they splashed and snorted. Later we dried in the sun, dozing to the sound of the horses grazing contentedly nearby. At night we crept from the bunkhouse and slept curled in deep straw under the watchful gaze of a gray mare or, for me, my favorite roan.

In those carefree days of my adolescence, I often dreamed of my own metamorphosis, of feeling my hands seeking the ground, my feet hardening to hooves, of tossing my head back and feeling my hair spread around my arching neck, of suddenly breaking into a gallop across a field, whinnying to the other horses resting together under the moonlight, of moving in among them, my muzzle outstretched, softly blowing and drinking in the scent of their warm coats. Even years later, when I hear the word *horsewoman,* my mind conjures up some mystical creature part horse, part woman. I see her rearing up on sinewy haunches, gleaming coat blending into smooth alabaster skin, a mane of glistening black hair filling the air around her.

So much about horses reminds me of women. Both are innocent yet beguiling, delicate and strong at the same time, with a tempest brewing behind soft eyes. Both are prone to basking in attention and apt to show great displeasure when passed over, social to the point of distraction, and gentle and kind in nature. Both are easily frightened or driven to worry, surprisingly steadfast and resourceful when cornered, and stubborn to a fault, yet eager to please those they favor. And both possess a flair for the dramatic.

Perhaps I feel an affinity with horses because I recognize in them parts of my own feminine nature: a strong sense of intuition, a deep desire for community and safety, and an occasional desire to run kicking and squealing without cause. In the presence of a horse, I feel drawn into a primal conversation that does not involve language or training but that is based simply on raw emotion. That feeling may not be unique to women, but I know that when I've communicated with a horse, I have felt a connection unlike my relations with any other animal or person.

During my school years, I became more interested in the horse as a living organism. I was fascinated by the inner workings—the tissues tying bone to bone, blood as it coursed through ancient veins, maturation, and parturition. There was nothing about the horse that I didn't feel a need to know. I worked for veterinarians, breeders, trainers—anyone who seemed to have a key to understanding the beneficent beast. At the racetrack, I ponied races and exercised horses, counting the pounding heartbeat beneath my legs, feeling the lungs expand and the muscles explode into action. I watched the eyes and ears of the young horses as I ushered them past the stands to the gate. As a technician, I stared at their spun blood under the microscope, memorized the tissue layers of gaping wounds, and waited patiently outside stalls for urine samples. As a college student, I learned about embryology, nutrition, and genetics.

Interestingly, the veterinarians I worked for were mostly men, my professors in college were predominantly men, the trainers and breeders I knew—men. Yet 68 percent of my graduating class at Michigan State University was female, and the year I applied to veterinary school more than two-thirds of the applicants were women. Every riding school where I have either ridden or worked has been populated mostly by adolescent and teenage girls. A visit to a local fair, show, or sanctioned horse event reveals that the vast majority of competitors are female. It has always intrigued me that there are more men at the professional levels of the horse industry (veterinarians, farriers, trainers, jockeys), yet statistically more horses are owned by women, and women consume more products within

the horse industry. Of course, in recent years we have seen women commanding the highest level of our equine sports: a recent Olympic jumping team was made up of all female riders, and dressage has been dominated by women at the international level for years. European teams are showcasing more and more female riders. Women now outnumber men in veterinarian programs nationwide. Still, the disparity cannot be denied: women tend to be the consumers in the horse industry, while men tend to be in roles that provide services.

I have to surmise that horsemen gain great satisfaction and reward from their involvement with horses, just as women do. I also can bear witness to the fact that many men in the industry are capable of tremendous compassion and unabashed love for their horses. One top corporate executive I know is quite fond of singing to his horse!

Still, there is something about the relationship between a woman and a horse that seems deeply reciprocal. I am certain, at least in my case, that I get far more from my horse than I give—and let me tell you, I give and give! Most of the horsewomen I know would even say that they don't just *want* horses in their life, they *need* horses in their life. When it's time to pay the show fees and the veterinarian bills, I just smile and think about all the money my horse saves me on therapy and medication and gym memberships.

Perhaps for some people, dogs or cats provide the same sense of well-being. I am a dog person as well and adore my two Jack Russell terriers to the point of embarrassment. I also spent several magical years as a zookeeper and had some extraordinary relationships with a variety of species (in particular a golden eagle, a South American douroucouli, a toucan, and twin giraffes). Each one offered me unique glimpses into a spiritual place I have not experienced elsewhere. Nonetheless, when I see women and horses together, I see something greater at work: I see how strength and power can coexist with patience and compassion.

In my animal massage practice, I see horses in a variety of mental and physical states. They are often ill or injured when we meet. Other times they are geared up to race or to show, and like any athlete, they have their game faces on. Frequently, they are old and wizened and facing their final days. What never fails to amaze me is the way they are always open to receiving aid and the way they participate in their own healing by being present in the moment.

I am often asked if it requires exceptional strength to massage horses; outward appearances would lead you to believe this to be so. In fact, I find that it requires less strength and leverage to massage horses than I often need to work on people. I attribute this to the horse's natural tendency to "be there" with me. Horses are free to receive without the distraction of future obligations or the burden of past transgressions.

I am not surprised that the majority of students in my massage courses are women. As natural caretakers, we have an amazing sense of how to help, whether the horse's needs are physical, psychological, emotional, or as most often is the case, a combination of the three. I have also found that horsewomen have an open-mindedness and a sense of wonder that the horse immediately perceives, and often that allows the horse to do the teaching.

The horse-crazy girl is alive and well inside me even after all these years. I still get goose bumps when my horse nickers and rushes to the gate upon seeing me. I am not sure why this causes such a strong visceral reaction in me. My dogs fawn over me every day, leaping and rolling at my feet, which makes me ecstatic. My husband and I start and end each day with a kiss, without which I would be lost. My girlfriends and I are given to declaring our undying friendship while passing toilet paper under stalls in the public bathroom (usually after a few glasses of wine). But all this pales in comparison to having a 1,200-pound animal call plaintively to me from his stall when he hears my voice. Is it a maternal pang that I feel in my chest at that moment? I think part of the charm is that the horse's response is completely voluntary (he gets fed whether he calls to me or not), entirely contrary to his genetic wiring (I am a meat eater after all), and thoroughly selfless. In today's world, we can use all the selflessness we can get.

*I have worked with or trained more than 3,000 horses.*
*Every one of those horses has surprised me, if only in a small way. And I have learned something from every horse I have worked with or trained. How many horses does it take before we can understand this animal? Is it possible that horses are so multifaceted that knowing them is beyond our reach? Are horses that complex?*

*I ask these questions because it would seem that people should be more complex than a simple creature such as the horse, but I am not finding this to be true. I have spent far more time studying horses than I have studying humans. I claim to have such expansive knowledge of horse behavior that I have based a career on it. In an average year, I teach 250–300 students and their horses how to interact in a more harmonious way. Almost without exception, the students respond exactly the way I expect them to; from their horses, I learn something new. I ask a question of a student and can usually predict the answer. I ask a question of a horse, and it is anyone's guess how the horse will respond.*

*I think that the fundamental difference between people and horses is that horses live in the present while people can call upon and consider several different options before responding. We make decisions based on history, the present situation, and expectations of the future. We almost always want to be predictable, to fit in, and to please the teacher. Horses make decisions based only on the data that is available at the moment and are not concerned with the images they are broadcasting. This is not to say that horses do not remember their pasts, just that they do not depend on them quite as much as we would like to believe to make their decisions.*

*The person who is "great" with horses is not the one who can memorize their body language better but the one who can adapt to the here and now as well as a horse can. It does not matter what a person can remember about horse behavior, but rather how proficient that person is at responding immediately to the questions and answers that the horse gives her. If a person gives the wrong answers or takes too long to answer, she loses credibility in the horse's eyes.*

*The horse is simple, but it is this simplicity that we have difficulty with. Horses make hundreds of rapid-fire decisions daily based on the here and now. People, being more complicated, base decisions on a myriad of data. To give the "correct" answer, a person comes up with a response that is based on what she knows or believes to be true (history), what is in line with the image that she wishes to portray (present), and what puts her in a position to improve her status (future). Because a person has more data to consider when answering a question, the number of matching responses is reduced. Only a few answers will match all the criteria of this complicated equation, making a person's answer easier to predict. The horse, by contrast, relies only on the present situation for a correct answer, allowing for many possible answers.*

*There is one other piece that may make this puzzle easier to understand. I have never worked with a horse who refused to make a decision. No matter what the question, horses always give an answer. Some people can put off making a decision for years or lifetimes.*

# AN ARTIST'S SIGHT

*by Dawn Frinkler*

*O thou, my milky-white pony,*
*whose coat is as the moon-beams*
*of this autumn night, carry me like*
*a bird through the air…*

—Muasaki Shikabu (974–1031),
*The Tale of the Genji*

*Her eyes grow* large and round as her jaw begins to fall. She barely inhales and is almost afraid to breathe or blink for fear she might miss something. She looks around in awe and wonder, almost as if she cannot believe her eyes. She may cry or begin to laugh, she's not sure. She is no longer aware of anyone around her who could be watching, nor does she care. For her, there is no one or anything else that exists for that moment.

What I have just described for you is the reaction of every young girl around the age of eight who approaches my display of paintings. It is almost always young girls, very rarely boys. I never tire of seeing the beauty of the connection girls have with horses as they are drawn to the expressions and personalities in my art. This relationship of the heart is unique, unlike any other—a relationship made up of faith and belief without the necessity of proof.

I cannot take my eyes off of horses. I love watching them, their grace and majesty. They bring to me a calm quiet, a belief that good and pure exist in the world, that life can be untainted, uncorrupted, and that I am accepted for who and what I am.

To begin to understand the relationship between horses and women, one must first understand what we share. There is a unity, respect, peaceful understanding, and quietness between us. When I look upon a horse, I see him for who he is, not as an object or a trophy. I look upon a horse, and I feel a union between us that begins with the loss of all time and place and ends with feeling whole and at peace.

Many seem to believe that a horse's energy needs to be harnessed through control. I debate that if you share a horse's energy through a bond, it will last forever, whereas control lasts only as long as the moment. The idea of possession through control is merely superficial. There is no greater beauty than what one possesses inside; know the horse and all he has to offer, become one with him. It is not sexual. But it is intimate and elemental.

I once had an art instructor who had us take exactly one-half hour to eat one teaspoon of rice, and then we were to write about the experience. The entire purpose of this assignment was to teach us about "seeing." If you cannot see something or feel it, then you cannot translate it into art, nor can you respond to it in any other manner. This quiet learning is one of the ways that women understand horses so well. It's about savoring every moment and every experience with a horse and learning from them all. It means taking the time to truly experience the moment.

I learn every day, as much as I can. What I notice in life is that people don't really know how to see. And maybe I notice this so much because I am an artist. Women tend to be more insightful than men, which may explain much of the frustration that we feel at times with our significant others. This is also a primary reason that women have such a bond with horses. Women are patient with life,

they listen, and they see what many others overlook.

The relationship between women and horses is an intuitive search revealed as a natural bond built through the sharing of life. I am fortunate to be able to share with the world what I "see" in horses. When I paint, it is as if I get to breathe life into horses and return to them the beauty they have shared with me.

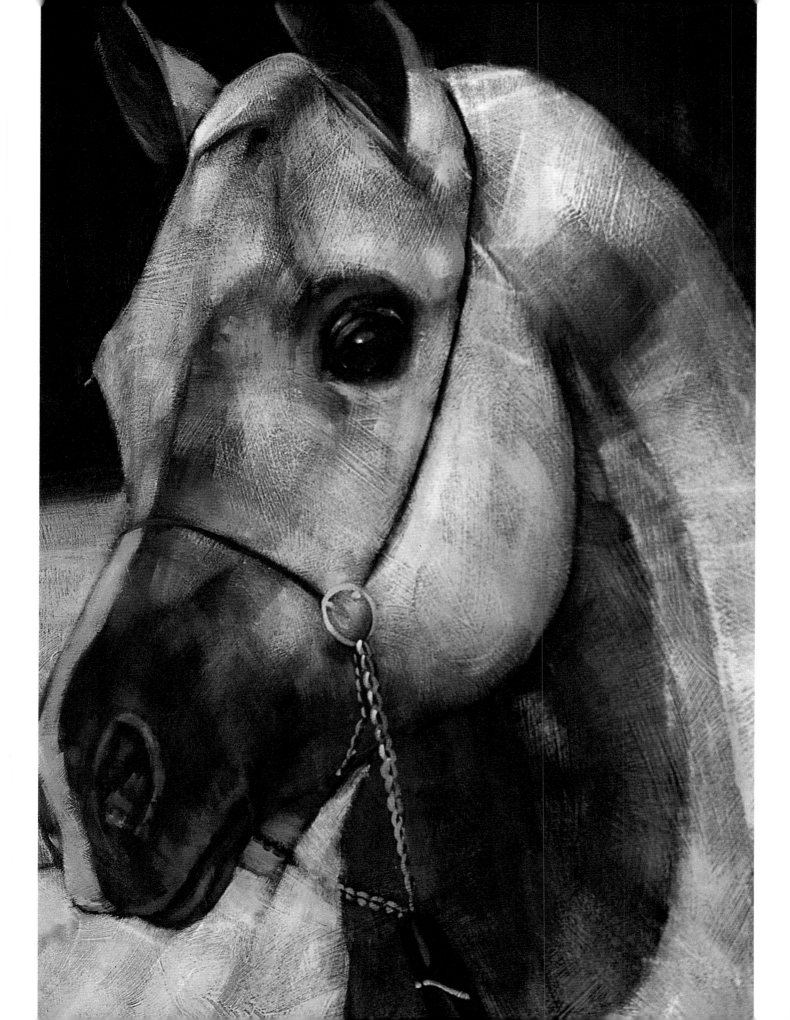

# THE SPIRIT OF THE HORSE
# CAPTURED BY A SPIRITED ARTIST

*by Liliana Gomez*

*When Allah created the horse*
*he said to the magnificent creature:*
*I have made thee as no other.*
*All the treasures of the earth shall*
*lie between thy eyes …*
*Thou shalt fly without any wings,*
*and conquer without any sword.*

—The Koran

*I was born* and raised in Colombia, South America, a country in which the passionate love of horses has lived since the beginning of time. My Aunt Laura gave me my first opportunity to be in contact with these magnificent animals. Aunt Laura practiced jumping, and she decided that my mother had to go to every tournament she was competing in. Aunt Laura was convinced that my mother was good luck because she won every time my mother watched her compete. I was a young, spirited girl around eight years of age, and I gladly attended each of these exciting events.

I vividly remember the huge impression those beautiful, gigantic animals had on me as a young girl. I felt intimidated and could not be too close to them, but I fell in love with the horse's splendid outward appearance. Sometimes I was in awe as well as a little frightened! As soon as I returned home from these trips, I was always in a hurry to take a piece of paper and begin painting horses. That was the moment I discovered I was good at imagining horses everywhere: jumping, galloping, and even flying in freedom! Thus I began to transfer my feelings of awe and excitement into an art form.

That childhood experience signaled a direction that would weave its way through my life. With my mother's initial introduction to the world of the horse firmly established, my father, a doctor with an enormous passion for the arts, continued to nurture and support my budding artistic talents. My father had hundreds of books about art, and he also collected canvasses of various sizes as well as an assortment of tools, oils, and acrylics; and paintings would emerge. I spent many hours very late into the night watching him paint his ideas. As a youngster beginning my first horse drafts, I tried to imitate his

unique artistic process, which he created specifically to express his emotions. My family and friends showed me much respect and attention, which was most encouraging to an "emerging young artist."

My mother enrolled me in every art course she could find to develop my talent. When it was time to go to university in Paris, I had explored many different aspects of art, my favorite being art history and literature. In university, while studying oil and acrylic techniques, sculptures and ceramic, and the basic concepts of drawing, I always had horses in my mind. Upon graduating, the first thing I did was set up my studio and begin experimenting in pastels, human figures, and portraiture. One day, a lady came to my art studio and asked if I could please paint some horses for her. *Finally*, I thought, *a commission to do something I am good at!*

I committed all my energy to this project, and I tried to combine my classical training with some of the unique ideas and techniques I had inherited from my father. I imagined what it would be like to be galloping along on a real horse: fast, exciting, pulsating energy—and a little fear. Some of my technique came from my own ideas of freedom and my dreams for the future. As my paintbrushes splashed onto the canvas with such gusto, I felt myself flying with my imagination into a world where horses go. Using acrylics and texture on a large canvas, the end result was fantastic!

This was a turning point in my career, and in time a close relationship emerged between my painting style and the spirit of the stallions. I began to study different kinds of horses: their breeds, their histories, as well as their heritage. I especially enjoyed learning how they have been sharing and contributing to the building of our world, participating in battles and conquests. History teaches us how men have transformed the horse's anatomy. Every type of job has affected horses' muscles and sizes. This gave horses an unusual variety of shapes that is an enjoyment to sketch. Two breeds especially caught my attention: the Arabian horse, with its unique contour and powerful design; and the Andalusian, with its strength and variety of color reflected by the sun.

As I enjoyed success, I decided to continue to work hard with my own ideas and visions about horses, feeling so honored for being able to turn their essence into paintings. My exhibitions brought my art to many people in my native Colombia. I was encouraged by their responses, knowing so many others felt the same way I did about the heart and soul of the horse.

Another turning point came as I understood I could communicate my feelings to the rest of the

world. Thankfulness welled up inside of me, and for the next ten years I continued to work hard at my craft, adding other elements and materials to my canvas. Over time, my style has changed and matured, achieving a distinct visual impression.

When I moved to Canada with my family, I discovered many more breeds and colors of horses. Such variety! I also rediscovered a special magic with the eye of the horse: it reflects life! We see the nobility and a little of the ingenuity of these spirited but shy creatures. The paintings come alive as we see this remarkable reflection from this incredible animal.

I am currently getting up close to my equine models as I photograph them for portraits with their owners. It is always exciting, exhilarating, and sometimes a little nerve-racking for me. I remember the awe and wonder I experienced in their presence as a young girl, and I feel honored to be able to capture their magnificence on canvas. While I paint many subjects using many styles, my favorite is still the horse!

# ESCAPING WITH EQUINES

*by Margo McKnight*

*A good feeling after the ride is
better than winning a prize.*

—Bertalan de Nemethy (1912–2002)

*For me, horses* represent an escape for me. As a kid, they were an escape from the regular routine of "kidhood." The sense of mobility and the ability to explore the farthermost corners of the planet, or a neighborhood, was possible with a horse as my companion. As a youngster, I did not own a horse. So my steeds were borrowed, rented, plastic, wooden, and most often two-dimensional. I loved to draw them.

The most typical escape for me was poring over paper with pencil, drawing for endless hours my favorite subject, the horse. My horses had rough lives. They lived in deserts and jungles, they thundered away from lions, tigers, and wolves. They were always muscled and long-maned, with unusual markings. They were wild. They never got caught. My pencil drawings allowed me to live with horses anywhere I chose.

I also collected plastic figurines of horses. In the "ice age," long before Breyer horses, these plastic figures were my equivalent of dolls. My plastic herd did not like tack. I tried unsuccessfully to scrape the bridles off, which led to bad scarring. So my story was that the barn burned, and the horses escaped but not without scars from their bridles, which had caught on fire! Drama figured predominantly in my horse world. My passion for horses also caused a bit of consternation and outright fear in my family. I would seem to be possessed by the spirit of the horse and cavort around on all fours, bucking, running, snorting, and drinking from troughs (aka cereal bowls). I would respond only when addressed by my chosen horse name, Duchess, which also doubled as my dog name—but that is another story. At school I was called "Horse." I chose to believe it was because of my equine obsession and my unruly frizzy long mane.

My sisters thought there was something seriously wrong with me. They complained to my mother, a nurse, and my father, a teacher. Both parents educated and trained to deal with patients and children reassured my sisters that I was not a whacko and explained that many kids have make-believe parts to their lives. It was not until my father's seventieth birthday celebration, when the family gathered to reminisce and tell stories, that the truth was exposed. My parents had actually been shaken by my extreme bouts of equine role-playing. To avoid scaring my sisters, they placated them with the bravado of parental knowledge. Wow, I had no idea.

I carried the visual arts into my high school years. Although the subjects of my art had now expanded to include Joe Jackson and Bob Seger, a natural progression no doubt, horses were still on my list of favorite things. My interest in conservation biology began to emerge as I learned more about the plight of

the natural world. Then my interest in nature turned into a panic of how to save it. As I began to fantasize a career in saving the planet, the horse came with me. After a brief search for the appropriate vocation, I realized there was no degree in "Planetary Savoir-ism." Forestry seemed a good option. I would live in the woods, ride my horse to my fire tower, and let the pony graze below while I scanned for fires. I would fill in the time drawing and painting. Upon investigation, I realized that fires are an important part of many ecosystems, but horses and forests are not the best mix. I settled for a basic zoology degree with an inordinate number of electives in fine arts.

Stang, the mustang, was my first real-life horse. I was twenty-two, a bit of a late bloomer in the girl/horse world. I was working as a graphic artist and a freelance artist and was a full-time student in Tampa, Florida. I needed a wonderful distraction that would help me forget the deadlines, the professors, and the structure of my life. I needed Stang. I shared this ungainly steed with my best friend, Lise Elkin. Lise and I were warned about this bad horse. "He will wait until you are relaxed, then he will run away with you . . . you can't stop him . . . that horse can run for hours with a man on his back . . . he will kill you" came the words of warning from a man who had had some experience with this horse. The mustang was cheap, however, so Lise and I drove out together to visit this brutal animal. We rounded the bend to the ranch where he lived to see a young girl standing on the back of this nice, sturdy-looking chestnut gelding with a blonde mane. We forked over the one hundred bucks and drove home with giant smiles and grand adventures planned.

Stang was a great horse. He was not beautiful, well trained, or smooth-gaited, but he was solid, hardy, and afraid of nothing. He had an odd interest in mail-

boxes, but other than that quirk he was the best first horse two twenty-two-year-old females could have had. We did not have enough money to buy proper tack for him, so we invested in a bit and bridle but rode him without a saddle. Our plan was to save up money to get a good one. By the time we had the cash, we were used to the feel of no saddle so we never bothered to acquire one. Stang did like to run. You just had to know how to ask him to stop, and he would.

Lise and I often wondered what Stang's life had been like in the wildlands of Oregon, where he had been rounded up. We both felt a bit honored to own him. The one hundred dollars seemed an insult. Stang died at the age of twenty-six at Lise's house in Land O' Lakes, Florida.

The second horse I owned was a crazed Arab mare whose name I changed to Chronos, which means "time." Time is what I needed, and Chronos was the horse to deliver it. Riding her allowed me to slip into wild places, leaving the glow of computer screens far behind. A ride on this gray mare through oak hammocks and pine flat woods was no walk in the park and forced us both to focus on the moment. She would pop in the air at the sight of an armadillo, of which there were many, and stop dead in her tracks from any speed for a gopher tortoise. My focus during our rides was 100 percent, and the escape from all else was 100 percent as well. Chronos also forced me to make her my priority. She did this quite cleverly by injuring herself with frustrating and expensive regularity. In the few years that I owned her, I lunged her, wrapped her legs, and groomed her far more then I ever would get to ride her because of her penchant for injury.

I boarded her down the road from my house at a barn owned by two wonderful women, Kathy and Angie. These women taught me patience and how to wrap a leg in five seconds flat. When I accepted the job as the director of the Brevard Zoo on the east coast of Florida, I left Tampa, and I gave Chronos to Kathy and Angie. They were both emergency medical technicians by training. I thought it only appropriate. Chronos helped me leave daily stress where it should be and move into her world. My next horse is going to be a big, gentle quarter horse gelding that does not mind armadillos.

I am again using the horse to escape. This time, much as when I was a child, it is the two-dimensional horse that is drawing me in. For the next two years I am focusing my art on the form of the horse. I have recently taken on the task of illustrating a book on equine massage for Lola Michelin, an exceptional horsewoman and massage therapist for humans and horses—as well as a giraffe! For me, reconstructing the horse on paper, layer by layer, muscle upon bone has been a wonderful exercise. It has changed my equine paintings dramatically. Although I am not moving through the natural world on the back of a magnificent creature, I lose myself in the process of capturing the image on paper and canvas—perhaps the greatest escape of all for me.

I am lucky. For me the horse is an escape—not my core work or my industry but sheer pleasure of form and function, something I admire and sometimes get to ride on, photograph, paint, or simply stand near and breathe in deeply. I believe the natural world is critical for the well-being of humans. Our dependency on animals both wild and domestic stretches far beyond the ecological processes. Some of us are just more dependent than others or are just lucky enough to have known a horse.

*I am thrilled that Margo McKnight is included in this book.* We met five or six years ago when I was filming an episode of Jack Hannah's Animal Adventures at the Brevard Zoo. Margo was director of the zoo at the time, and I was impressed upon first meeting her. Later, after getting to know her better, I realized that she is a true advocate of animals and the environment. (I don't use the word advocate lightly. I consider very few animal lovers, environmentalists, or activists to be true advocates of the animal kingdom.) My second introduction to Margo was a couple years later at the same zoo. I was invited to be the keynote speaker for the opening of its Africa exhibit, and I jumped at the chance.

Close friends know that I spent my childhood planning for my future career as Marlin Perkins, the host of Mutual of Omaha's Wild Kingdom. I figured that by the time I was old enough to host a weekly television show, viewers would be sick of watching Marlin and I could slip right into the cast. I started grooming for the part at age nine or ten. The first step was to memorize all of the factoids on the backs of the Mutual of Omaha animal card set. Needless to say, I probably have more factoid knowledge pertaining to warblers, water buffalos, and wombats than anyone you know—and that is just the Ws.

At age eleven or twelve, I had the opportunity to work at the Terry Lou Zoo for a summer. This is where the female chimpanzee named Mike, of The Merv Griffin Show fame, made her permanent residence. I was sure that knowing and caring for her would in some way impress those who would be hosting future casting calls for my television debut.

Later that year, a friend and I opened our own zoo. We charged fifty cents per admission and had the most complete collection of North American turtle species on display in the United States—that we knew of. We had even begun our first research project. I had noticed that the majority of female box turtles we collected had brown eyes while the males were an even split with 50 percent having brown eyes and 50 percent having red. We had not read anything in any of the herpetological papers that even suggested eye color had anything to do with sex. I was never published, but in an informal way, I am still conducting my research. If you are ever on a trail ride with me and you see me dismount to pick up a turtle, you will know what I am doing.

Our zoo was not open for very long. We convinced only seven or eight people (including parents) to pay admission, and shortly after opening, our star display was stolen by some neighbor kids. Jaws was a twenty-two-pound snapping turtle who was "trained" to snap at a broom stick and snap it in half, demonstrating to the crowds how powerful a snapper's jaws are.

At about age fourteen, my piano lessons turned into a rock band, my Roger Conant field guide was traded in for a synthesizer, and I spent the next ten years pursuing the more realistic career of a rock star. Back down to earth, I pursued my gifts for understanding horses, which brought me right back to where I started, pursuing Marlin Perkins's job. I do not know if I am any closer now, but at least I get to hang out with people such as Margo McKnight and Jack Hannah.

# HORSES FOREVER IN MY LIFE

## by Lynn Palm

*I will not change my horse with any that treads on four pasterns . . . When I bestride him, I soar, I am a hawk: He trots the air; the earth sings when he touches it; the basest horn of his hoof is more musical than the pipe of Hermes.*

—William Shakespeare (1564–1616),
*Henry V* Act 3, Scene VII

*Ever since I* can remember, I've loved horses. I believe that I was born with this gift, a consuming passion for the horse, because no one in my family had horses and nobody instilled this in me as a child.

I was born in Philadelphia and spent my earliest years in the little town of Kirkwood, New Jersey. Although I was raised in a completely "nonhorsey" family, my neighbor did have horses. One of my earliest memories is of standing at the window and looking out at the little red barn across the street. In the paddock was a black-and-white pinto pony named Sweet Donner, a little sprite of a pony who officially started my craze for horses. Like so many young girls infatuated with horses, I started collecting everything that had anything to do with horses, and to this day I still have some of my first Breyer models.

When I was six years old, my father's business took our family to Florida, where we settled in Sarasota. To my total delight, we moved into a neighborhood of minifarms and horses. I immediately started begging my parents for a pony, since we now had an entire five acres just waiting for an equine resident. Of course the one I chose, a bay grade mare with a pretty head and Welsh breeding, happened to be in foal. I named the mare Sugar, and when her foal was born, a filly with a flaxen mane and tail, I named her Honey. I still have my first saddle, a little western saddle I got with this pony.

As fate would have it, just four lots away from home was a small farm with a red barn painted with white trim. It had Dutch doors and all the paddocks had white fences. It had the look of the perfect picture-book farm, and I was smitten.

After school and on the weekends, I rode my bike past it in hopes of seeing someone on a horse. I saw a lady riding, and apparently she noticed me, because after a number of visits on my bike, she asked me to come in and see her horses. This casual introduction was how I met Ms. Bobbi Steele, a truly talented horsewoman. Although I had no way of knowing it at the time, I would spend years studying and riding under her instruction, and her guidance would influence my career with horses in many ways.

To the horse-crazy girl I was then, Ms. Steele's life story was like a fairy tale. Born and raised on a farm in Illinois, she had run away from home at an early age to ride in the rodeo. Later, she joined the circus and became a performer. In the late 1930s and early 1940s, Ringling Bros. bought animals from all over the world to perform in its circus acts and hired trainers from points near and far. Ms. Steele was hired as a rider with Ringling Bros., and for at least a decade she made the circus her life. She rode with German trainer Captain William Heir, learning dressage to its highest level and a broad repertoire of tricks and circus movements with horses.

After Ms. Steele left the circus, she continued performing, doing her own exhibitions at major horse shows across North America. She traveled with two horses she had trained herself, a Thoroughbred and a saddlebred. Among her remarkable acts was one in which her horse was standing at liberty and, when called, would come up to and jump over Ms. Steele and the stick she was holding.

I met Ms. Steele after she had retired in Sarasota. I was eight or nine years old; I never really

knew how old she was. All I knew was that she wanted me to start riding with her. My parents never had to pay for a lesson, so I did anything I could to help around her farm. Whenever I had a question or needed help with my own ponies, Ms. Steele was there. She was my mentor, and she introduced the whole world of horses to me. She always emphasized that the principles of dressage could be applied to any breed of horse and to any discipline, something I still practice today. This training gave me the basis for the training I went on to do with quarter horses and the success I've had in the show ring.

I rode at Ms. Steele's farm for six years before she thought I was good enough to enter a dressage show ring with her horse Knick Knack, who was half quarter horse and half saddlebred. He was just three when I started riding him, and Ms. Steele trained us together. I remember one summer I did nothing but sitting trot circles, learning how to collect the horse and set his head, learning how to get him more balanced as he advanced in his training. When I was a teenager, I bought a grade mare named Mocha Dell and trained her with Ms. Steele's assistance. I did my first bridleless routines with this mare.

By the time I was in high school, my parents had accepted that I was determined to follow a career with horses and that college wasn't part of the plan. Graciously, they took the money they'd saved for college and allowed me to attend my senior year of high school at a private school that had a riding program. After I graduated, Mocha Dell and I got a job at Frontier Town, a Wild West–style tourist attraction in North Hudson, New York. We performed three shows a day, seven days a week, and even learned to do some trick riding.

Although I did my first bridleless routines with Mocha Dell in those early years, it was with the amazing quarter horse stallion Rugged Lark that my bridleless exhibitions really made an impact. Rugged Lark and I started performing together after he won his second AQHA Super Horse title. We began doing bridleless routines set to music and ended up performing at many major shows, including the National Horse Show, AQHA World Championship Show, the Quarter Horse Congress, and even the 1996 Olympics in Atlanta. Every exhibition I did, I thought of Ms. Bobbi Steele. A perfectionist, she was always a performer, never a competitor, so she was always in the limelight. I learned that as a competitor, you had to win to be in the limelight.

Ms. Steele passed away on my birthday in 1983; I will always be indebted to her in countless ways.

Another important horsewoman who has had a great influence on my life is Andy Mooreman. Back in 1969, she got me interested in registered quarter horses and the AQHA. She gave me some jobs right away, and she helped me get my first registered quarter horse. She was a wonderful mentor to me and continues to be a respected horsewoman. Her forte was teaching and coaching, and it remains so to this day.

When recognizing mentors, I must mention Carol Harris. Carol believed in me as a trainer. She was a great influence and support, and she trusted the training and competing I did with hers and other people's horses. And I would be remiss not to mention Rugged Lark. An outstanding teacher doesn't have to be human. Rugged Lark made it crystal clear to me that the better I rode, the better he would perform. He taught me invaluable lessons about building a special partnership with a horse.

I've been fortunate to have won a record four AQHA Super Horse titles (more than any other female competitor), thirty-four AQHA World and Reserve World Championships, and numerous European championships during my career. Although I still love to compete, my focus has now changed somewhat. After Rugged Lark retired from his regular public exhibitions in 1997, I directed my business toward coaching and educating riders. I have always both taught and coached, even while I had my own heavy competition schedule, but today, my energy is focused more on education. I've had success, and I want to give back to the industry that's been so good to me. Teaching is nothing new to me. Even as a teenager I was giving riding lessons to the neighborhood kids. I find great reward in working with, and influencing, riders of all ages, but especially young riders.

Women are in the majority of the many riders I teach at my farms in Michigan and Florida, and I think this is because women are a major part of the horse industry at every level. Women are caretakers, and we thrive on the responsibility of caring for our horses. For those of us who never had children, our horses often become like our children. We also have great compassion for horses, and I think this is tied in with the female psyche.

All through my career with horses, I've seen how they bring out the best in people, especially women. I also think it is our responsibility to bring out the best in our horses. Caring for my pony gave me a sense of responsibility at an early age. As I learned more, horses gave me the desire

to achieve something with my passion. The more I practiced my riding, the better I got, and this spilled over into other areas of my life, including schoolwork. As a teenager, being busy with my horses kept me out of trouble. Although during those years I also participated in other sports, there came a point when I was so busy that I realized I had to choose something to focus on. No doubt about it, my decision was to focus on my horses and riding. I'll never get bored with horses. As Ms. Steele always said to me, "Horses are a never-ending learning experience!"

Horses have taught me what I needed to succeed in life. Whether I have good days or bad days, my horses have always been there for me. My life revolved around them as a young child, and now decades later, it still does.

# FOLLOW YOUR HEART

*by Pat Roberts*

*The rider casts his heart over the fence,*
*the horse jumps in pursuit of it.*

—Hans-Heinrich Isenbart,
*The Kingdom of the Horse*

*I fell in* love with horses from the moment I saw my first one. How could a little curly-headed two-year-old, who couldn't even look a huge animal in the face, develop such a long-lasting love affair with the horse? This is one of the mysteries of life—the love affair between female and *Equus*.

Lucky for me, most of my father's family lived on ranches. As I grew up, I spent my summers and vacations on my cousin's dude ranch, which was also a working cattle operation. When I was seven, my grandfather gave me a small, almost black, unregistered three-year-old gelding called Poncho. This was the first horse I could call my own. On weekends until late in my teens, Poncho and I roamed the Corral de Tierra hills near Salinas Valley, where I was raised. Then we traveled to Jamesburg in the upper Carmel Valley to work the summers taking care of the city slickers who came to ride the rugged mountains between Big Sur and the Jamesburg area. I consider my childhood ideal: I had a loving family who allowed me the time and the opportunity to nurture my relationship with horses. I knew deep in my heart that what I wanted most was to be surrounded by horses.

My life as a central California horse-crazy girl certainly did revolve around horses and horse-related events. One of my earliest memories is of riding in the Salinas California Rodeo parade on a gentle horse being led by my father on his cowpony. And while growing up, I watched with interest a young man by the name of Monty Roberts who lived on the Salinas Rodeo grounds. Raised by parents who taught riding, it was natural for Monty to enter the family business; he did around age seven.

Monty and I attended the same grammar and high schools. I guess it isn't surprising to anyone that we gravitated toward one another and onto a path that led us into a relationship that has taken us to places that neither one of us could have imagined.

Until the time of our marriage, my only goal was being around horses for the pleasure their company gave me. After marriage, I stepped into a new role—I suddenly discovered the joy of competition and fell in love with one horse in a way a child normally falls in love with his or her first horse. Her name was Julia's Doll.

Julia and I had the most wonderful four years together in the show ring, and that has set the show standards for me ever since. I had the incredible experience of falling in love with a true champion. Julia was an elegant, dark brown mare who moved like silk on the rail. She earned many championships in pleasure classes, had the athleticism to be able to change leads with every other stride, and was beautiful enough to win numerous grand championships at halter. Together we made her an AQHA champion, which meant she had to exceed at both halter and performance. What more could a young woman want? Julia and I had almost twenty-six years together, first in the show ring, and then later as she became a successful broodmare. Her granddaughters and grandsons are in our fields to this day—her lasting legacy.

After Julia came Holey Sox, a champion cutter who taught me so much. More and more I spent time on the back of my beloved friend. My children all inherited love for the horse, and there were years when it was such great fun to haul all three children, along with their respective steeds, to the junior shows and watch them develop as individuals.

During the late seventies, horses took on a new persona for me. Judging conformation, structure, and correctness of limb became more important in my life than ever before. Developing an eye for these characteristics helped me choose yearling Thoroughbreds to develop into two-year-olds for the racehorse market. Watching these animals move at the walk, the trot, and the canter was like a university education for me, but "graduation" came in a very different way than I had ever envisioned: I never thought that my accumulation of knowledge about equine conformation and movement would lead me to become an artist.

Suddenly I found that I had stepped into a new role and expanded career. Sure, I had doodled on scratch paper, sometimes horses and sometimes people—but become an artist? With children grown and more time on my hands, I began to paint; first landscapes, but eventually my heart drew me back to the horse. Then came the decision that for all time has changed my life, my decision to create my horses of bronze.

One cannot imagine how many ways there are to tell a story about a horse, even in bronze. I've shown the world the camaraderie of a horse and dog, the antics of a young horse rocking and rolling on his back, a mother with her foal standing on shaky legs. I've created the buckaroo and his cow horse, a vaquero and a California cowboy with his trusty quarter horse and cow dog off to do their work. The movement of wild horses in flight, the magnificence of Andulusian-warmblood crosses standing on their hind legs—all have been inspirations I have used to "paint" my pictures in sweeping bronze strokes.

My creation the *Moment of Join-Up* has given me recognition as an artist beyond my greatest dreams. This sculpture depicts the moment in time when a wild horse decides to Join-Up with my husband, Monty, because of a bond between them forged through nonverbal communication and the horse's understanding that Monty is to be trusted. *Moment of Join-Up* is in Windsor Castle in the collection of Her Majesty, Queen Elizabeth II.

Shy Boy is another horse who will be forever remembered in bronze. He's a wonderful little bay BLM mustang Monty adopted so the BBC could create a documentary of a successful Join-Up with the added challenge of accomplishing this on twenty-two thousand acres instead of the normal fifty-foot round pen used in domestic situations. Shy Boy has been the subject of two bronzes to date and quite appropriately so. He will never be forgotten because he is the mustang who goes into studios with Monty to help PBS raise funds for outstanding television programming about animals and other family-oriented subjects. Shy Boy (who is really not so shy) has been the focus of two documentaries and one book and was an equestrian participant in both the 2003 and 2004 Rose Parades. I proudly rode Shy Boy down the streets of Pasadena. Not once did he falter as the crowds of more than 1 million people thronged, yelling and clapping. He took it in his stride like the star that he is.

There have been countless other equine personalities I've enjoyed immortalizing, such as Quincy Feature, a beautiful chestnut quarter horse stallion who was twice World Champion at halter and an AQHA Champion, and who was another

labor of love for me. "Feach" was beloved by all those who knew him. His strength of character and other significant attributes needed to be chronicled so he would never be forgotten—even though his legacy of outstanding progeny gives everyone reason enough to remember him.

Horses, both real and created, have given me the opportunity to travel to Dubai and other such unique cultures. I have exhibited my bronzes in Europe, met artists from faraway Russia, Germany, Spain, Rumania, and Turkey. Horses have given me far-reaching recognition as an accomplished artist, friendships with royalty, and the excitement of travel to far and exotic places.

Follow your heart and your dreams will come true.

lesley harrison
© psa

# AN ARTISTIC EQUINE JOURNEY

*by Lesley Harrison*

> *With flowing tail and flying mane,*
> *With nostrils never stretch'd by pain,*
> *Mouths bloodless to the bit or rein;*
> *And feet that iron never shod,*
> *And flanks unscar'd by spur or rod,*
> *A thousand horse—the wild—the free—*
> *Like waves that follow o'er the sea—*
> *Came thickly thundering on.*
>
> —George Gordon, Lord Byron (1788–1824),
> *Mazeppa*

# Making a living in the

arts has never been an easy task for anyone in America. And yet, succeeding in the arts remains the dream for so many aspiring actors, writers, musicians, sculptors, and painters. Perhaps you are one of them. If so, take heart, there is hope.

For as long as I can remember, well-intentioned people discouraged me from pursuing a career in art painting horses. They assured me that I certainly would not be able to succeed as a pastel artist, and a woman artist at that! Now how is that for a few challenging mountains to climb? Well, I'm proud to report that for more than twenty years I have been making a wonderful living as a pastel artist painting, as you would guess, horses.

The "experts" who told me I would never be able to succeed as an equine artist didn't realize that their words would be motivating to me. I'm not sure why the word *can't* motivated me so much. It could simply be because I'm a stubborn Taurus, or maybe it's because of the temper reflected by my reddish-blond hair. Or perhaps it's because I was blessed to have a wonderfully supportive family. With their encouragement, I've always thought I could be and do most anything! My mother has never believed in the word *can't*. Given her way, she would have it struck from the English language. It's a good lesson for all of us who have challenges to embrace and mountains to climb.

One of my favorite quotes belongs to Rumi, who said, "Let the beauty of what we love, be what we do." My life has always revolved around animals, especially horses. And since they are now a big part of my daily work as an artist, I have a wonderful excuse to be surrounded by them in every way, every day. I have a studio at home where my own animals share the space with me. And, of course, I have horses.

Creating a new painting is an experience from the very beginning. Sometimes when I see a horse at a show or in a magazine, I will call the owner to ask about the possibility of painting the horse. That often means traveling to people's ranches or stables, meeting those animal lovers, and hearing the stories they so lovingly tell about their special animals. It is at this time that the emotional part of the painting actually begins. Seeing an animal, looking into his eyes, touching him, and watching him move are all things that affect me emotionally. How can they not? So with sketchbook and camera in hand, I proceed to go about accumulating the needed reference material for the painting. Then it's back to the studio to begin the actual process of putting concepts onto paper.

Designing the painting is the hardest part for me because it always involves making tough decisions that inevitably affect the success of the final painting. Trying to decide whether to paint the horse in a field of flowers, in the snow, in the water, or in a pasture must be confronted. The question is always: What will best complement the animal and make for the most pleasing and most emotional painting possible? Then it's hours and hours of being alone. Horses are so beautiful yet so difficult to paint correctly. Painting for me is usually peaceful and frightening at the same time; I always want the painting to be the best one I've ever done.

When a painting is finished and if I'm really satisfied with the emotion reflected in the final outcome, it's truly a great feeling! And what a privilege it is then to watch the public response to the image as it is translated into a different form and becomes a print or a gift item or used on the pages of our calendar. For me it is one of the most gratifying feelings of all because it allows the work to be shared with so many more people than the original painting could otherwise touch or reach. In many respects, my artwork, my career, and my dreams for being a successful equine artist have all been about sharing.

Being a painter can sometimes be a lonely profession, though the work and the images are always shared with others in one form or another. After years of painting at home, I got tired of never being able to get away from my work, so I rented a studio space in town. An advertising man with a small marketing agency leased the office suite above me. He brought his dog to work with him every day. He still loves to tell the story of the first time I was in his office.

It was beautifully decorated with Oriental rugs, leather chairs, and a huge desk. And on that desk he had three or four polo magazines with a pair of polo spurs on top of them. He tells people that I said to him, "Do you play polo, or are these just for display?" I'm not sure if I said it quite that way, but I do remember at the time I was positive that they had to be there just as decoration. So I was wonderfully surprised when he said that he indeed played polo and loved horses! I remember rushing to the stable to tell my friends the news. I had met a very handsome, single man who loved horses and knew how to ride! Not just ride but also ride well enough to stay on a polo pony. And this is where I began truly sharing my art and my career with him and with so many others

That man and I have been married now for almost ten years; we have joined our lives both personally and professionally. He's the "Keller" portion of Harrison-Keller Fine Art & Gifts. Horses remain an important part of our lives. We have had some phenomenal horse adventures together, and all of those adventures have had a profound influence on my art and my work.

We've been to Montana numerous times to help friends who own a huge cattle ranch. The summer cattle drives take seven wranglers and three dogs a good two weeks to move fifteen hundred mother cows and their babies up into the high country for summer pasturing. We spent from twelve to fifteen hours in the saddle each day. It's hard work indeed, but what an opportunity to inject some firsthand understanding and knowledge into my artwork.

One particular year my husband and I joined the same friends for the fall roundup and spent five days riding in the blowing snow, gathering cattle and bringing them down off the mountains. We really depended on our horses to get us safely through the long days in blizzard conditions. What teamwork and dependence upon one another. What a privilege to work so hard to get the job done with our horses, dogs, friends, and oh so many snow-covered cattle.

We have friends who live in Wyoming, and we've been privileged to ride their horses all through the public land and national parks, including the beautiful Teton Mountains outside Jackson Hole. We've been with wild mustangs, ridden in the high country, and seen moose and grizzlies from horseback. We've raced through the surf and slept under the stars, listening to the coyotes sing; we've saddled up in the dark and watched the sun come up on horseback. Yes, Rumi, you can say it again, "Let the beauty of what we love, be what we do."

I really do think that all of these experiences, plus having owned horses for most of my life, are a big part of what contribute to each painting. Isn't a painting, after all, just a wonderful attempt to capture a moment of life, a moment in time, and preserve it forever? Those elusive and sweet times in our lives seem to rush by us so quickly. I only hope that my paintings can freeze-frame some of them forever. Most are just too delicious to forget.

My journey as an equine artist has been a special one indeed. As we travel with our work, we encounter some phenomenal stories. Some of the stories are about horses, and just about all of them involve people who love their animals very much. There have been a few stories that have touched me deeply.

For example, I was once given permission to choose any horse or horses I wanted to paint at an Andalusian breeding farm. There were more than eighty to choose from, so I felt a bit like a child turned loose in a candy store. As I walked up and down the barn aisles looking in the box stalls, I was stopped in my tracks by a certain stallion. He was beautiful and tall and exuded such a special presence and had such an extra something. I had no idea at the time that he was totally blind.

We were told the story about how at the age of two he severed his optic nerve and became instantly blind. With courage, confidence, and love, he went on to be competitively shown and is now one of the farm's main breeding stallions. He is totally dependent on his handlers and trusts them implicitly. If he gets nervous when he is taken out of his stall and walked around the farm, his handler says "I've got you," and he visibly relaxes. If they're going over uneven ground or have to step up, the handler says to him "step up." He immediately starts walking in place and lifting his front legs higher than normal to be able to negotiate whatever is coming his way. What profound lessons are to be learned from him, and what great gifts he continues to give to all who are around him.

Another amazing story is of a deaf paint mare whom trainers weren't able to work with because she was skittish and completely frightened of just about everything and everybody. She was born deaf, and in her quiet world spent most of her time sleeping. Her owners loved this mare, and she caused them tremendous worry. They finally came up with the idea of asking a mutual friend who trains horses and who is also deaf if

she would try training the deaf mare. You should see the two of them together. There is a bond that they alone can understand, and it would move you to tears to watch them. The deaf trainer has taught the deaf horse how to respond to hand signals and to look at her constantly for signals and reassurance.

What a privilege it is to witness these amazing real-life stories and then be able to go back to my studio and try to paint what I have witnessed. What a privilege to attempt to tell the horses' stories, stories about love and understanding and courage and trust. They become stories that require not a single spoken word, only the stroke of a pastel stick on paper to convey their tender and emotional message.

Mine has been an artistic equine journey filled with challenges, hard work, plenty of satisfaction, and, yes, a great deal of wonder. I grew up loving horses and have never stopped. The blessings I have received in return are beyond words, and perhaps that's why I paint. And if a picture is truly worth a thousand words, I hope my art speaks volumes to those who love horses as much as I do.

*"Let the beauty of what we love, be what we do."*

*Imagine what would happen to our species if all of us understood and practiced the wisdom in that statement. Notice that the quote does not say, "Let the beauty of what feels good, be what we do," but rather "what we love." I think this is a very important culture-changing difference. I think this is one of the clearest differences between our current society's way of thinking and most indigenous peoples' mindsets.*

*Focusing on what feels good keeps us here in the temporal while focusing and acting on what we love moves us into if not the eternal then at least a multigenerational way of thinking. I thought for a moment about what our species might be like if we spent time on what we love rather than what makes us feel good.*

*The first thing that comes to mind, for me, is our children. Assuming that we love them more than anything else, what would happen if we let the beauty of our children be what we do? I am reminded daily, as I pass housing development after housing development, that we love how we can make our kids feel more than we love our kids. I know that the idea has become almost cliché, but why can't we comprehend that our time is so much more important to the next few generations than swimming pools, central vacuum systems, Xboxes, and ballet lessons? Sure it is nice to be able to provide those things for the kids, but would it not be better to provide the things that they need first, and then provide the things that make us feel good? Actually, wouldn't it be better to provide the things that they need rather than sacrifice those things for the things that make us feel good? I can remember saying to my own kids, "You don't appreciate everything that we've done for you," "I work all day, and you don't appreciate all of this stuff!" Now I understand why kids do not appreciate all of that stuff: because none of that stuff is important to them, it is important to us.*

*What is important to them? Having us spend time with what we love, doing the things that they want to do, whether it be playing in the sandbox (without our watches on) or setting up the Breyer horse collection for the thirtieth time. They tell us what is important; we're just not willing to listen. The first thought that comes to our adult, responsible mind is, "I can't spend time with him all day; someone has to go out and earn the money for all of the stuff that we have decided to own." Wrong answer! Kids really do not care how much the house costs, they really do not care if the car is brand new or ten years old, and they really do not care if you scoop ice cream or design software. How much space do they need? Exactly as much space as is in the fort that they make out of sheets and kitchen chairs.*

*Am I ranting? Forgive me. Look at your floors, your furniture, your wine glasses, your cars, and think about this: How much time did it take you to get all of those things that make you feel good? Where would you be if you had spent all of that time working on what you love rather than what makes you feel good? Lastly, if you add up all of the hundreds, maybe thousands, of hours that you spent working on things that are supposed to make you feel good, rather than working on things that you love, how good do you really feel?*

121

# THE HORSE IS A MIRROR TO THE SELF

*by Peggy Cummings*

*Show me your horse and
I will tell you what you are.*

—Old English saying

*Even as a* young girl growing up in San Salvador, I understood that horses teach us lessons about ourselves and how we relate to the rest of the world. Over the past twenty years as a rider and a clinician, I've watched women learn how to communicate better, find validation, increase their self-esteem, become empowered, and develop mastery over themselves and their lives, all through their relationships with horses. These gifts and skills become an integral part of their lives and transform the way they interact with human as well as with equine partners. To me, the essence of the relationship between women and horses is the tiny miracles that happen every day that help women overcome the fears, insecurities, and limitations that keep them from becoming their most authentic selves.

We are rarely taught communication skills as children, so our abilities to communicate effectively with other people as adults are often limited. We don't always understand that different perceptions and disparate backgrounds can create miscommunication and misunderstandings. Our major way of communicating is with words, but communication is more than just speaking. It also involves validating and understanding the other and feeling validated ourselves. This is what a horse asks of and offers us: validation and understanding. We do, of course, use our voices to communicate with horses, but how we use them makes a big difference. Toning, changing the inflection of our voices from higher tones to lower tones, for example when saying *easy* or *slow*, is very soothing.

Yet a horse communicates primarily with his body, not with words, so we must learn to do the same. We must not only develop our use of body language but also improve our body uses as well. We learn from our horses to use our inherent listening, feeling, and observing skills in new ways so we can create reciprocal partnerships with them. Our hands may connect with the horse, but it is through using the whole of ourselves—thinking, feeling, sensing, acting, hearing—that we can truly feel the nuances that speak to us through the horse's body and his movements. It is then, and only then, that we can translate this into fluid movement in both horse and human. We learn from horses to use our inherent listening skills in new ways so that we can forge relationships with horses. By being patient and listening with our whole selves, our minds are open to finding creative ways to invite the horse to participate with

us. This opens the way for communication between a woman and her horse.

The horse is like a mirror of the human being. When we are tense, horses reflect our tension. A reactive horse's behavior escalates, whereas the more placid horse shuts down. The horse is constantly reacting to the human and challenging her to be a better communicator and a better partner. When women learn to observe and listen to the horse, we are continuously reminded to be the best we can be, not simply in the ways we use our bodies but also in our behaviors, our attitudes, our focuses, and our thinking. By being quiet and present in ourselves, we invite horses to reciprocate, opening the way for trusting communication.

When women who have not communicated as effectively as they would like with fellow human beings start to feel a connection with a horse, they begin to open up and seek that contact with other human beings. This is so powerful. Women start seeing the correlation between the ways in which they react to the horse and the ways they react to human beings. Previously unsuccessful and limiting patterns are changed, and women then can focus on growing and improving themselves.

Working with horses also gives women a feeling of empowerment that makes us feel good about ourselves and imparts a sense of safety. We can observe the horse's behavior and make decisions about where we want the relationship to go. We can engage the horse in a conversation, create a dance of movement, and take a journey together that is reciprocal and fulfilling.

When a woman feels capable of engaging, feeling, participating, and making choices, she develops her own sense of self. She becomes more independent and doesn't rely on others to tell her what to do. It is a beautiful thing to watch a woman recognize that value and take that knowledge out into the world.

Like horses, people experience a flight or fight reaction to perceived danger and fear. When we are in a reactive mode, our emotions drive our behavior. This mode limits our choices in the moment. Working with frightened horses offers women the opportunity to learn how to choose a different response. We can learn to work through the fear, bring ourselves back under control, and have more choices in potentially dangerous or stressful situations. It is only then that we can bring ourselves back to safety. We can reengage the horse by breathing deeper and using the natural rhythm of the body to relax and reconnect.

With these techniques, a woman reassures both herself and the horse, and the fear cycle is broken. The women I've worked with take this very important message and apply it to every aspect of their lives. They learn that in any situation that compromises their safety, the best thing to do is use the tools of connection to find options that bring them back to safety. That's a valuable life lesson.

Women crave intimacy, deep friendship, a partnership in life. Horses allow us to experience these connections even when we cannot find them in our human interactions. I've worked with hundreds of women who didn't understand this until they started riding! The feeling of being heard and understood by the horse paves the way for a woman to expand her relationships with people.

There is a special community and a kinship among horsewomen because of our shared love of horses and our constant drive to improve our relationships with them. I've seen how this common bond encourages women to open up and share with one another. In the horse community, women experience validation both from the horse and from each other, and this confirmation gives women the spirit to test themselves and their abilities both as riders and as human beings. The powerful feeling that comes from being heard, understood, and accepted gives women wings of courage.

Women have an intuitive sense about what will and will not work when communicating with a horse. Horses validate this intuitive sense by giving us direct feedback without personal attack. This two-way communication cultivates our sense of being seen and heard. We then begin to believe in ourselves and our contributions, which builds our self-esteem.

I have watched thousands of women connect with a horse and learn to have faith in themselves and their abilities. They take this same self-esteem and lead happier, more fulfilling lives as a result. This is the most powerful thing I have ever experienced as a woman and a clinician. When women stop blindly following the "experts" and begin to create their own opinions, their own feelings and ways of assessing and understanding a horse, something truly magical can happen in their lives.

And then there's mastery. Mastery is really, truly knowing something inside and out. It's learning something so well that your competence is unconscious, yet you can still bring it to your consciousness. It's simply a part of you.

Horses teach women how to have mastery over ourselves and our lives. Horses teach us where our strengths lie and where we need to learn more by asking us to set really clear boundaries, to be very specific, and to trust ourselves. They teach us what our capabilities and our limitations are. Feeling validated, clear, strong, and empowered from learning gives us a strong sense of ourselves. To know these things about ourselves gives us mastery over our lives.

I don't just observe these lessons in others. I've learned these lessons firsthand from my teacher Scotia, a thoroughbred Percheron who has been my mentor for twenty-two years now. He created the roadmap that took us on an amazing healing journey.

He came to me as an unstarted five-year-old. When we began unloading him from the trailer, he was afraid of backing down the ramp. He panicked and came out the escape door, badly injuring his hind legs and hips. It took a year for him to recuperate before I could begin riding him. Without the ability to speak, Scotia painstakingly guided me to communicate with him in a way that kept us safe, strengthened our bodies, and renewed joy in our partnership. That experience taught me to pay attention to his body language and to listen for the nonverbal clues to help him heal. Our dressage training had caused us both relentless physical discomfort and mental frustration. When I got tight and stiff in my body, he got willful and rigid in his. We were not having fun. When I learned to relax and let Scotia's movement come through my body, allowing motion in all my joints, his movement became fluid and he was happy in his work.

His confidence in me, his unfailing patience, and his trust have given me the self-confidence to continue my work, to bring these lessons to others. The most important lessons are to consistently release tension and bracing out of my body and to rebalance through movement. When I feel rigidity in the horse, I add rhythm and movement, many times imperceptibly to others. The horse feels this support and allows me to guide him into freedom of motion and self-carriage. This learning has brought mastery into my life and into other women's lives. Scotia's most profound teaching is that life offers an infinite number of opportunities to learn, heal, and continue our journey if we just keep our focus on our goals and our dreams.

Over the past twenty years, I've been privileged to see women take these "horse" lessons into their everyday lives and use that knowledge to improve their circumstances, heal their souls, and develop options that are empowering for them. Horses give women the tools to healthier, happier, more rewarding lives. Who could ask for more?

# BOUND BY BEAUTY

## by Karen Brenner

*My Beautiful! My beautiful!*
*that standest meekly by*
*With thy proudly-arch'd and glossy neck,*
*and dark and fiery eye,*
*Fret not to roam the desert now,*
*with all thy winged speed…*

—Caroline Norton (1808–1877),
*The Arab's Farewell to His Steed*

# Women and horses:

what is the bond that ties? Just as every being is unique, the relationships between horses and women are unique as well. My love for horses is built foremost upon admiration of beauty. John Lyons says that horses are God's favorite animals. They are definitely the most beautiful He created. They are amazing to watch, whether they are quietly grazing, playfully running through the pasture, or patiently waiting for their evening scoops of grain. There is a beauty about horses that no other animal possesses. Now I admit that for some, appreciation of beauty may be subliminal—even ignored, denied. I wonder why.

As an artist, capturing beauty is my goal. Creating work that is beautiful—so obviously beautiful that it can't help but be noticed—is what I continually aspire to achieve. It is a lofty goal, which I will happily strive toward, hopefully, for many, many years to come. And what better subject to depict than horses? They are already beautiful!

What bonds others to the horses in their lives? Is it awe of freedom, power, strength, and energy? Yes. Is it unconditional friendship? Yes. Is it love? Yes. How about the continual opportunity to learn new things about horses? Yes!

And then there are the bonds with horses that go beyond the explainable, formed in a spiritual moment—a connection of souls—that happens when you least expect it. Your eyes meet with a horse's and a current of understanding flows like a jolt of electricity; a bond between two beings that is unexplainable, unexpected, undeniable. In that instant you know, no matter what, you will always be connected.

Have you ever felt that same electric spark when awestruck by the beauty of a sunset, a babbling brook, a wildflower swaying in the breeze, a herd of wild horses galloping free? Just being witness to beauty can create a moment of intense awe so overwhelming it creates a rush. Experience it. Feel the connection. It is a connection with God, the creator of all things beautiful. It is a bond that lasts forever.

How far away are you from beauty? I say as close as the nearest patch of woods, the nearest garden, the nearest child. Can you find beauty? It is standing in the nearest pasture waiting for a scoop of grain.

Horses let us accomplish things—great and small: to form lasting friendships; to be free, if only for a moment; to see beauty . . .

. . . to bond with God.

# FROM RIDER TO HORSEPERSON: A BREEDER'S TRANSFORMATION

*by Saret Tola*

*You can tell a horse owner by
the interior of their car.
Boots, mud, pony nuts, straw,
items of tack and a screwed-up
waxed jacket of incredible antiquity.
There is normally a top layer
of children and dogs.*

—Helen Thompson

# The night of

his birth came exactly on her due date. I was charged with excitement, although I was exhausted from my ten nights' vigil—awake, waiting, expecting, anticipating—in the camper parked near the barn. The foaling attendant with me snored softly on the couch while I listened to the baby monitor. Staring too long at the fuzzy black-and-white screen connected to the camera in my mare's stall played tricks with my mind, so I traveled back 345 days to the beginning of the process.

My plan was to breed my perfect riding horse, so one winter I went looking for his mother. I had peoples' voices ringing in my ears: "Buy a foal, something already on the ground." I was looking for THE mare to bring him into the world, and then I found her. Jeté was a striking, harmonious Holstein mare who was considered lesser stock because she was not over 17 hands. When I touched her, an instant surge of well-being came over me: through Jeté's eyes, I could see her heart. I knew she was a wise old soul, patient and calm, although only four years old.

Needless to say, I believed in that mare, and I gave her a loving connection with a human, something she had not known before. While Jeté was being bred, I pictured, constructed, willed the colt who was my heart's desire. I formed him in my mind. I knew the curves of his body, the color of his coat, his kind eye, his spirit. I even named him: Balta'Czar. I had Shakespeare's words from *Venus and Adonis* swimming constantly in my mind:

Round-hoof'd, short-jointed, fetlocks shag and long,
Broad breast, full eye, small head and nostril wide,
High crest, short ears, straight legs and passing strong,
Thin mane, thick tail, broad buttock, tender hide:
Look, what a horse should have he did not lack,
Save a proud rider on so proud a back.

All at once the rushing water I heard brought me back to the present as I saw Jeté crumple to the soft straw in her stall. I bolted out of the camper. I think my heart grew wings and carried me over to the laboring mare. *No slow down, don't disturb her.*

I heard the horse across from her nickering assurances. My eyes jumped to Jeté, to her hind end facing me. A wave of guilt passed over me as I thought that I was directly responsible for her current condition and possible imminent danger. The

knowledge that a very small percentage of foalings result in difficulties was a small comfort.

A yellowish bag ballooned out, and I charged back to the foaling attendant, but I couldn't wake him! About two eons passed before we both returned to the straining mare. I could see a hoof. *Oh I knew it!* The white markings were there. My entire being was with the mare and the baby being born. I was electrified, feeling as though I were being born again, too. Somewhere in the background I heard the foaling attendant say, "Call the vet! We have a head back. CALL THE VET! We have a problem." It was as if I was struck by lightening. All I could see was white, my breath coming too fast, I'm tingling. *Hold on, Saret,* I said to myself, *you memorized the vet's number. You can do this.* I stared down at my phone, but I was blank. The only number I could remember was a dear friend's so I called her—at 2 a.m.

My voice in her ear: "Jeté's having her baby—call the vet—there's a problem. A dystocia! Hurry!" Thoughts that dystocias are life-threatening to mares *and* to foals wavered through my mind and made my feet unsteady. I had to force myself to walk back into the barn. My eyes wanted to avoid the stall in the middle, but my connection to Jeté and her foal was too strong. I looked, ready to see a steaming lifeless form with expressionless eyes. But the foaling attendant was experienced and quick. His arm inside the mare found her colt's head in a dangerous position. With a seemingly synchronized movement of a human arm and an equine contraction, out came the head, neck, and shoulders of the baby.

My being became incredibly light, my heart soared. There was Balta'Czar—alive! His dam gently nickering the first hello. The hind legs weren't even born yet, but the rest of him was there shivering, not from cold, but because his nervous system was starting up. As I leaned down next to him, he whinnied a shrill, urgent baby hello, and I knew that this was the best night of my life.

Oh, the joy of a newborn foal! Being a breeder and standing stallions offers me the chance to share in the enchantment and wonder of a newborn foal again and again. Our mare-owning clientele who have foals by our stallions excitedly share their experiences, so I am fortunate enough to relive this moment with each foaling story told. For each woman, becoming a foal's human matriarch cultivates and satisfies our nurturing, motherly instincts. By nature, newborn foals are skittish and untrusting of humans. Once people interact and gently restrain a young foal, we can change his behavior toward us so that he comes to understand his human as caretaker, safety zone, teacher, disciplinarian, and a constant presence in his life. Witnessing a foal's trust in humans grow is one thing that compels me to continue breeding. Throughout my horse-human interactions, this trust that begins at such a young age, expands and deepens, leading me to the truest connection I have experienced between equine and human.

I was a rider, then a breeder, now I am a horseperson. At first, I thought the way to the closest relationship between horse and human was to buy a three- or four-year-old horse not yet schooled under saddle. Has my thinking evolved! Missing out on the first three years of a young horse's life denies us the foundation on which to build the strongest relationship possible; it deprives us of the chance to mold the colt or filly's mind with ours, prevents us from truly knowing each other.

True, the road from insemination to mature horse is a long one, indeed, but we humans cannot buy trust from horses. This incredible journey demands the time, creativity, and patience it takes for real trust to form. Working with young horses every day of their lives educates me in the myriad questions and answers between human and horse. The ongoing trials and tribulations of teaching seemingly simple tasks such as haltering, leading, trimming, blanketing, tying, trailering, solidifies the horse-human relationship. Funny enough, the more I teach the young horses, the more I learn from them. During the hours spent working with young horses, I have actually become the student learning how my horses' minds work, how they are going to react, and what their individual sensitivities are. This reciprocal relationship, starting at foaling and extending through maturity, opens the door to an elevated connectedness experienced between horse and rider throughout under saddle work and higher training together.

The fulfillment that I feel from the relationships with my homebred warmblood horses drives me to be completely passionate about breeding. How many times have I heard people say that breeding takes too long, is too risky, not worth the time and money, results in too many unknowns? None of these worries holds true for me now. Becoming ravenous for more information about breeding led me to research bloodlines and conformation of warmblood sport horses. My knowledge was further increased as I spoke with as many respected (and patient!) warmblood breeders as would put up with my incessant, pestering questions. I ordered and pored over books about warmblood breeding and in-depth histories on bloodline matches, or nicks.

I began making a yearly pilgrimage to Europe to see firsthand these outstanding horses who have been bred for sport for hundreds of years. And the result? I became enlightened about how to "load the dice," to produce a foal more aptly suited for dressage and/or jumping. As my knowledge increased, the quality of my foals continued to advance. Now I feel it is my duty to pass along my knowledge and experience to other people seeking it. My goal is to help the American-bred warmblood sport horses develop the consistent high quality that the European sport horses possess.

The life of a breeder involves working seven days a week, twelve-plus hours a day in 30 to 100 degree weather, numerous sleepless nights waiting for mares to give birth, living in old T-shirts and jeans but sturdy paddock boots, never going to bed before grabbing the flashlight to check on the well-being of the horses, and never ever being able to have a vacation. Is it worth it? Well, this question is answered every day when I am on the back of my now six-year-old homebred stallion, Balta'Czar. When I have just barely thought of a question to ask him and he has already responded, when I know what he is going to do before he actually does it, when I can touch him and know where his mind is, when I see his beauty as great on the inside as on the outside, the payback for the years of work is right here.

*Toward the end of her essay, Saret talks about her* homebred stallion Balta'Czar as if he knows what she is thinking as she is thinking it: "When I have just barely thought of a question to ask him and he has already responded, when I know what he is going to do before he actually does it, when I can touch him and know where his mind is, when I see his beauty as great on the inside as on the outside. . . ." Is it possible to have this kind of relationship with your horse? Absolutely yes! There is a price, however.

A close friend, who is also a bit of a sage, sent some wisdom my way recently while we were enjoying supper together. He said, "Pony, you can have whatever you want, but you can't have everything, and there is a price for whatever you choose." Maybe it is just my current situation, but those words rang very true, and I have tried to remember them daily.

Picking apart his statement brings up some interesting thoughts. First, he said, "You can have whatever you want." This might be the most important part of his statement because if we do not believe this part, the rest means nothing. If I say to you, "You can have whatever you want," what determines if you believe me or not? I imagine history, preconceived notions, self-esteem, and your general attitude toward life would play a huge part in your willingness to believe this statement. You might require "blind faith" or "a leap of faith" to believe the statement, but I would argue that the faith does not need to be "blind" at all.

My friend did not say, "You will have whatever you want," he said, "you can." This means that if you want the chance, you can have whatever opportunities you like. What you do with those opportunities is entirely up to you. Believing that you have the opportunity to succeed is the beginning of selecting exactly what it is that you want.

Next comes the most difficult part: deciding what you want. As you are deciding, remember the disclaimer at the end of my friend's statement, "you can't have everything." The lyrics of a Rush song read, "If you choose not to decide, you still have made a choice." The biggest obstacle that I see my students face within their horsemanship is failure to identify their goals. I can say, without hesitation, "If you want your horse to respond as lightly and intuitively as Saret's Balta'Czar, you can have it."

Next, there is the price. Are you willing to pay the price? Do you have the spare hours in your budget? Are you willing to sacrifice? There are no wrong answers. If you are willing to put forth the necessary effort, go for it! If you are not, it is OK. Make a decision to do something else. Just don't do what I see thousands of horse owners do regularly; don't require a certain level of performance without being willing to work for it, to pay the price. This will always end in disappointment.

If you believe that you can have the horse-human relationship that you are looking for and if you are willing to pay the asking price, there are no limits to the intimacy you can experience with your equine brother or sister.

# TWELVE FOREVER

*by Katie Upton*

*Blind with love, my daughter*
*has cried nightly for horses,*
*those long-necked marchers and churners*
*that she has mastered, any and all,*
*reining them in like a circus hand . . .*

—Anne Sexton (1928–1974), "Pain for a Daughter"

# What is it about women and horses?

My husband teases my horsey daughter and me that it must be a genetic defect. Though I have known men who are devoted to the world of horses, most of the truly horse-obsessed people I know are women. Whether we grew up around horses or didn't start riding until later (maybe much later) in life, the "horse gene" seems to affect us all in similar ways—we keep a horse in our heart, even if we can't keep one in the yard.

I was a really lucky kid. I've had horses all of my life and parents who not only tolerated my horse-craziness but actually supported it. One of my riding buddies captured perfectly what it means for us to be mature women in love with horses: "We're like twelve-year-olds with credit cards."

My mother thinks it all started when I was four months old at the Santa Barbara Fiesta Parade. She held me up to pet a horse's nose. When she tried to take me away from that horse, I cried and cried.

I remember my mom would sometimes let me eat my meals with my face, munching from my plate, chomping and snorting and tossing my head back and forth, flipping my bangs off of my forehead, glowing in my imagination. Perhaps I was a palomino that day, or maybe a wild mustang, I don't remember. But it was rare that I was ever anything but a horse. Children don't just pretend; they completely become what they love, with every gesture, gallop, and whinny.

There are many stories of my friends and me being horses. Even when we could ride our own real ponies, we would still sometimes prefer to be horses: bucking and kicking, galloping across the playground, jumping the lunch benches, combing our hair to one side so it would look like a mane. After school, we would canter across the Mission lawn, pampas grass plumes for tails, swishing all the way home. It was a serious thing—we weren't just playing—we were horses.

I started riding when I was three, and I got my first pony when I was five. I had three really close horsey girlfriends, and while we were growing up in Mission Canyon, we mostly rode our ponies together. We rode all over the backcountry trails, sometimes as far as the Santa Ynez River. We were always lost in our imaginations, our fantasy world somehow gently cradled by the natural world around us.

My friends and I had our first formal riding lessons from a crusty old cowboy. Actually, that sentence is a childhood memory—looking back, the lessons weren't exactly formal, and although he probably wasn't much past forty, we thought he was old. He taught us basic horsemanship and horse care. Maybe most importantly, he taught us to respect a horse's spirit, to learn from a horse, to think like a horse.

I don't remember when we became self-conscious, maybe in junior high school. Maybe if that had never happened, I would still be bucking and kicking and eating straight from the plate. My passion for horses is as intense and fresh today as it was when I was a child; it has simply taken on different forms. When I'm in my studio painting, I can't help but call on these memories of a life spent with horses. When I consider how special it is for a child to carry her passion unbroken into adulthood, I feel very fortunate.

And when I ride my horse, I am twelve again forever.

# PAINT HORSES

## by *Heidi Harner*

Under his spurning feet, the road
Like an arrowy alpine river flowed
And the landscape sped away behind
Like an ocean flying before the wind....

—Thomas Buchanan Read (1822–1872),
American poet

*A dream I* have had for most of my life is to have a horse of my own. Unfortunately that dream still seems to be a far-off reality since I currently live in a typical suburban neighborhood; my backyard is hardly big enough for my two dogs. My plans to eventually live in the country with horses have yet to be realized.

When I was a child, my family frequently moved from one air force base to another, so the prospect of owning a horse was completely impractical. To compensate for the impossibility of actual horse ownership, my mother, who had owned a horse named Bay River while growing up in the plains of North Dakota, gave me a book called *How to Draw Horses* when I was nine years old. I learned how to draw the basic pear shapes of a horse's body, head, and neck. I may not have been able to own a horse, but I was able to create any number of horses for myself in each of my drawings and paintings. Even after twenty-five years, I am still fascinated by the artistic contours of a horse's shape, the deep rich colors of a horse's coat, and the powerful musculature of a horse's body.

Many women share my unexplainable desire to be around horses and yearn to bond with these magnificent and graceful creatures. I have been able to partially fulfill my wishes to be with horses at the Museum at Prophetstown, a living history museum in Battle Ground, Indiana, that re-creates farm life from the 1920s. As the museum's resident artist, I have unlimited access to many beautiful Belgian horses. I love simply to observe their behavior as they relate to each other. I am able to photograph and paint the animals to my heart's content.

My association with the museum is one of several wonderful opportunities I've had that have enabled me to pursue my art career and my interest in horses. Recently, my family and I were able to visit the Nokota Horse Conservancy in Linton, North Dakota. The goal of the conservancy is to keep the rare Nokota bloodlines alive by breeding and selling the horses and providing a place of refuge. We spent most of the day with Frank and Shelly Kuntz, cofounders of the conservancy, meandering through the expansive prairies and mingling with the horses. For the first time I was face to face with a band of horses without a fence or barrier separating us. They were as curious about me as I was about them. They seemed to want to be near our little group of humans.

They let us touch their faces and long manes, but then, in an instant, they turned and galloped off, leaving us grinning in a dusty haze. At the end of the day, I was left to enjoy the five hundred digital photos I had taken. It was an experience I'll never forget. The Nokotas are now some of my favorite horses to paint.

It is nearly impossible to explain this affinity I have toward horses. It's a mixture of marvel and wonder, mystery and awe. When I paint horses, I am able to celebrate their beauty and convey my continual inspiration to my audience. I'm grateful for the people and opportunities God has given me, but in no way have I reached my destination as an artist. I will always have something new to learn and experience. I am enjoying this wonderful journey.

# A YOUNG LAKOTA WOMAN'S TIE TO THE *SUNKA WAKAN* (HORSE) NATION

### by Lisa Colombe

*The White Steed of the Prairies . . . was the elected [leader] of the vast herds of wild horses, whose pastures in those days were fenced only by the Rocky Mountains and the Alleghenies. At their flaming head he westward trooped it like the chosen star which evening leads on the host of lights.*

—Herman Melville (1819–1891),
*Moby Dick*

*In the Lakota* way of life, all natural things have a spirit. The eagle has a spirit, the Black Hills, our ancestors, the rock, the *Wakan Tanka* (Great Spirit)—they all have a spirit. Lakota people share a special relationship with all things natural and living; we are all related. For me as a Lakota woman who has always been raised with horses and within a horse culture, my relationship with the horse is something instinctive, personal, and spiritual.

I am Sicangu (see-chan-ghoo) Lakota. *Sicangu* refers to my tribe in south-central South Dakota, which America identifies as Sioux. The Rosebud Reservation is the headquarters of the Rosebud Sioux Tribe. *Sicangu* translates in the Lakota Language to the "Burned Thigh Nation." There was a fire long ago that overtook our camp. Many of our people burned their feet, legs, and thighs while escaping and fighting the fire. Other Sioux tribal bands started to refer to us as Sicangu from then on.

I come from a rodeo family. I grew up with the outdoors as my backyard. Horses have allowed me to participate in outdoor sports and have provided me with companionship. I have countless memories of my cousins and me racing our horses in the alfalfa fields and being lost in a three thousand–acre pasture, dropping our reins, and letting our horses lead us to Dad's horse.

My father's family (Colombe) has ranched on the Rosebud Reservation since the late 1800s, before reservations and fence lines existed. The Colombe family is a strong Sicangu family with cultural ties to the land. As a rancher's daughter, I spent much of my youth on horseback.

My mother's family (Bordeaux-White Shield) has a more traditional background. My mother grew up in the "Indian boarding school days." Most of the education available for Indians in the 1950s and 1960s was provided at Catholic boarding schools on the Rosebud Reservation. Therefore, my mother attended school fifty-odd miles from her home. In those days, our people were very poor; they did not have cars and jobs were scarce. My mother's family has always been focused on seeking and providing education to better our tribe's way of life.

My mother says they may have been poor, but only in money. She was rich in family. She recollects horses always being in her family. She has often told me of riding horseback with her siblings and cousins down to the White River to swim. She said they did not own a saddle and rode bareback wherever they went.

Recently, Mother was moving to her homelands and decided to return objects of my youth. I was excit-

ed as I rummaged through my collection of books and puzzles. I noticed every item was about a horse or was a horse. Horses have lived in my dreams since I can recall. I was then thankful to my mother, realizing that she had always supported my love of horses.

My experiences with horses have shaped me as a person, a woman, and an educator of children. I do not remember the first time I rode a horse, probably sometime when I was an infant. My first "horse" was an ornery paint Shetland pony named Wilbur. Of course, he was handed down to me after twenty cousins had ridden him. Wilbur was famous for knowing every trick in the book to get rid of his rider. I used to scare visiting kids by jumping on Wilbur bareback and being bucked around the corral. Then I would try to persuade the visitor(s) to ride Wilbur, too. I can't think of any kid who took me up on that offer.

My first real horse's name was Bear. Bear seemed enormous because I was only six or seven when I got him. He was the kind of kid-horse every parent looks for. I imagine he came from a horse sale nearby or from a neighbor. My younger brother and twin sister used to fight me over this horse. He was broke and would slow down if you were falling off. I learned how to ride on Bear. Ironically, when I was pregnant with my daughter, I needed a horse who was foolproof, and I purchased a horse also named Bear to breakaway rope on. This Bear is in the photos. He is a great old man.

There have been people in my life who have believed in me and strengthened my horsemanship and communication skills. For example, when I was about eleven years old, a lady named Judy Parker volunteered her time and horses when she found out that I was interested in barrel racing. She is one of the nicest people I have ever met. My grandma Vesta was a white woman, but other than her, there were no other non-Indian people in my family. Prejudice in small towns neighboring the reservation was obtrusive when I was young and is still present toward Indian people today. It was unusual to have a non-Indian woman want to help me. Not that I thought white people were bad; I just never knew of any cowgirl wanting to help little ol' me.

Judy helped me to learn the barrel pattern and to ride more confidently. She also helped me get over the fear of rejection by non-Indian people. I learned there are a lot of nice people of all colors and backgrounds out there. Other mentors of all kinds have since helped me become a better roper, barrel racer, cowhand, and person. I learned to open up and allow people to know me through my love of horses and desire to become an athlete.

Horses are one of the finest gifts to humankind. Lakota "way of life" means that a Lakota person strives to be the best family member possible, and when your family is taken care of, you strive to help your extended family and neighbors. My horses have always been a part of my immediate family. I respect their love and devotion to me. Horses help me remain happy.

I love to help family and neighbors. At the end of every spring, the cattle have to be rounded up, worked, and counted. We count to find out if all the livestock are present, in the neighbor's pasture, or missing. We ride our horses and move as many as one hundred to one thousand cows from a large pasture (somewhere between one and five miles) into a corral. We vaccinate the cows and brand the calves. To brand the 150- to 400-pound calves, we have a team of ropers on horseback, ground teams of calf wrestlers, a brander, a vaccinator, and a castrator.

On a particularly hot day when I was sixteen, I was helping my Uncle Tuck brand his calves—I was mostly wrestling calves teamed up with my cousin Ty. There were a lot of big calves and few wrestlers, so I started to weaken in the heat a little. Some teenage guys from the neighboring Pine Ridge Reservation came over to check it out, and they wanted to wrestle calves. These boys were supposed to be bronc and bull riders, I guess. Needless to say, it was a wreck. These boys couldn't flip a calf efficiently. I didn't know it but my grandpa showed up, he was pretty old, over 85. He never liked my being out with the men and boys—thought women shouldn't do that kind of work. The last calf left to wrestle that day was huge. The ropers usually save the biggest calf for last as a joke to the wrestlers on the ground, since wrestlers are usually getting worn out by the end. My cousin Ty and I had wrestled calves all afternoon and were watching as five of these Pine Ridge kids tried to get the last calf down. Then these young men let the calf go loose at the end of the rope with only one foot caught. Disgusted, I ran over there and grabbed the calf's leg while lifting him off the ground, and got him down and branded. My grandpa never said anything about my going along. I felt bad for the teasing the boys got out of it.

My relationships with horses have inspired me to continually seek knowledge of Mother Earth and Creation. I graduated from Todd County High School on the Rosebud Reservation in 1992. Then in 1997, I graduated from South Dakota State University with a BS degree in animal science. I hauled at least one horse with me wherever I lived or attended school.

Upon graduation from college, I worked for the United States Department of Agriculture in the Natural Resources Conservation Service. In January of 2000, I resigned from the USDA and moved home to the Rosebud Reservation with goals to help my people.

My uncle Dr. Lionel Bordeaux is president of Sinte Gleska (Spotted Tail) University, located near Mission, South Dakota. Dr. Bordeaux and the director of the SGU Sicangu Policy Institute offered me a consulting position in the areas of natural resources and agriculture. In 2000, SGU Ranch, of which I am the director, was founded for youth and their families to gather any information desired on land, natural resources, forestry, and related sciences—as well as to ride horses. Sinte Gleska University is a chartered entity of the Rosebud Sioux Tribe. We are in all ways a team. My experiences with horses had made me think that all young people should have the opportunity to explore themselves through relationships with horses. The Rosebud Reservation is a breeding ground for the youngest generation to reconnect with horses, develop a spiritual relationship with horses themselves, and, in turn, learn to value the earth beneath and around them.

With a few awesome volunteers and personal and donated horses, I started to research the need for horsemanship activities in tribal communities in the summer of 2000. We hauled horses to the tribal communities and advertised free horsemanship lessons. Kids came running down the hillsides. We definitely proved that not only do these little Indian kids love horses but also horses are the key to attracting kids back to the land. I continue to develop unique agriculture and natural resources projects for local communities and schools, with Lakota horsemanship and bison as the strongest components.

When I was a little girl and people asked me what I wanted to be when I grew up, I would reply, "I don't know, probably ride horses." Now I am grown up, and although I do not get to ride all day long, I still ride as much as possible. I continue to breakaway rope at

Indian rodeos in the Great Plains area of the United States. I also compete in the barrel-racing event when I have a dependable and competitive mount.

What I enjoy about Indian rodeos is all the people from all the other tribes. I feel good inside to be a part of this organization. I love to compete. I just picked up breakaway roping a few years ago. For this event, you basically rope a calf as in men's calf roping, only your rope is tied to the saddle horn with a piece of string and the string breaks from the horn when the rope is tight around a calf's neck. The fastest time wins, but usually you have to do this in less than three seconds to win money. I bought a horse and hit the road with a rope in my hand. I had always roped critters in the pasture and so forth but never seriously in the rodeo arena. Roping now has become my favorite thing to do. I started right out in the Pro Indian Circuit. I figured that I would learn pretty fast, and it feels great just to be there and compete.

Training horses has always been a passion of mine. I enjoy working with my own horses from the time they are colts till they are broke. I joined motherhood in January 2003, and that has slowed down the colt riding a little for the past few years. I don't mind. I now wonder why I didn't have a child sooner. I am looking forward in life to sharing my love of horses with my daughter, Vesta Jo. Vesta's daddy and my significant other, Jessy Carlson, is a professional horseman. In our opinion, he is the best horseman we have had the opportunity to meet. Jessy's support is awesome and key to my personal development as both a horsewoman and a woman.

I am the prodigy of a long line of tribal leaders, warriors, and ranchers. I have been using horses and bison to attract youth back to Mother Earth. Our people have been physically detached from the land

since colonial times and Ft. Laramie's construction, but the love and heartfelt feelings for Mother Earth are silently alive within each and every one of us Indians. I believe that my journey, or "god's mission," is to bring the horse nation back to my people. Horses are the key to our youth's accessing the land. By traveling across our lands on horseback, our kids are healing. I cannot express the extreme humbleness I feel in my heart to see them happy. That is why I teach. I suppose I was born to do exactly what I do. I am thankful for all the gifts I have been given, and I try my best every day to help others find their way, the Lakota way. My vision is to see my people doing well, with jobs and careers and smiles on the children's faces. Seems corny, I suppose, to some people, but I think horses are a sure way to reach people.

Horses sure have reached me.

*The elders say that the one thing that Indian children talked about more than anything else in the late 1800s was windows, clear panes of glass that could keep warmth in and keep bugs out. Glass was like the ice that covered the ponds in winter, yet it wasn't cold. It enabled you to see into another's home or vehicle, yet it trapped voices inside. The elders say that this was one of the first technologies introduced by Europeans that the Indian children envied. A move toward technology is usually a move away from tradition. For Indian children, it was a move away from horses. I raise this because Lisa's essay talks about bringing kids back into the horse culture and about using horses to reconnect kids with their heritage. I began doing what I do for the very same reasons.*

*I am often asked, "How did you get started in the horse industry?" or "What led you to write?" Although I had a pet horse when I was young, I never had any intentions of becoming a horse behaviorist. Beginning in high school, my intention was to wrangle the music business. I chose Berklee College of Music as my jumping-off point after turning down acceptances from several schools that would have allowed me to pursue a marine biology degree. After college, I traveled with a Native drum group for several years. During my "on-the-road" years, I became aware that many of the Indian kids I met knew very little about their history. At about the same time, I met a fellow who was making a decent living educating elementary and middle school kids about his own tribe, the Creek. His name is Jim Sawgrass, and we still see each other occasionally at powwows.*

*The movie* Dances with Wolves *was a recent hit at the box office, and it seemed like the time was right for me to present an accurate portrayal of history, bring Native kids a little closer to their ancestry, and rekindle my love of horses. That is how I met Kola. Kola is the horse featured on the cover of* Horse, Follow Closely *and has become a close friend and partner. He and I spent four years giving lectures at elementary and middle schools. Our busiest year included 140 different schools. In addition to the schools, I was invited to Indian educational programs all over the country.*

*The first time that I presented Native American Horsemanship to the children of a horse culture, I was astonished. Not only were these kids unaware of their own history, but also few of them had actually ever touched a live horse. I started the presentation a little differently than usual because I expected my audience to have a deeper understanding of the subjects I would be covering. I used phrases such as* as you know *and* of course. *After a short while, it was easy to determine that the hundred-plus Air Jordan–wearing kids didn't have a clue. In fact, the kids who lived outside Philadelphia had a better understanding of Native horse history than these western Plains kids did.*

*Since then, I try to take advantage of every opportunity that involves Native kids. Sadly, there are not many opportunities. Our government has spent over one hundred years doing a marvelous job teaching Indian children that the last thing they would want to be is an Indian child. Think about it: Native kids are no different from any other kids, and if given the choice, it is difficult for them to choose history over an Xbox. Thankfully, we have been given a teaching tool that is more mesmerizing than Nintendo, of higher status than Nike, and can be more addictive than drugs. We have been given the horse. Although our ancestors used the horse as a tool for war, we can use him as a tool to teach our children.*

155

Liliana Gómez /03

# THOUGHTS ON WOMEN AND HORSES

*by Laura Chapot*

*Horsemanship [is] as suitable
to women as to men.*

—Plato (427–347 BC), *Laws*

*From my early* childhood, I have always wanted to make horses my life. I could never imagine doing anything else. Because I came from a horse-oriented family, it was an easy choice. We have always lived on a farm so I have had horses around me since I was born; but my parents, both Olympic show-jumping riders, were determined to give my sister and me every opportunity to choose another hobby. We played tennis; took ballet, tap, and jazz lessons; swam; and twirled the baton; but riding always won out. So instead of working nine to five, sitting at a desk, and looking out the window, I spend my days working with the animals I love. The paycheck may be unpredictable, but the nonmonetary rewards are tremendous.

What attracted me to horses is probably what attracts most women. Unlike inanimate objects, horses think and feel. They respond to our actions, sense our emotions, and have the ability to give back to us in many ways. In addition to being a competitive person who loves the challenge of showing, I have the opportunity to work with horses, care for them, train them, try to figure out their problems, and see them improve. In the process, I form relationships with my equine partners. The emotional ties I form can bring heartache as well as great personal satisfaction.

Many women enjoy riding because it is a sport in which the whole family can participate. Everyone in my family rides, but we also help each other train and groom, and we lend each other support and encouragement. Everyone has a role, so we all celebrate when things go well. Even in families where not all members ride, there is plenty of opportunity to be involved.

Riding is one of the few sports in which people can participate for their whole lives. In fact, most riders at the top are well past their teenage years.

Success in all types of competitive riding relies on the ability to relate to the horse, assess different situations, and effectively communicate to the horse how to complete a task. Years of perfecting skills and dealing with different horses and situations make a rider better able to adjust training and strategy.

Success is achieved when horse and rider are of one mindset and work in harmony toward a common goal. A joint effort produces the best results. As with any team, if one player dominates or if there is friction among its components, that team can be beaten by one whose members are less proficient but work well together. A fabulous horse with a poor rider can produce good results, as can a brilliant rider on an average horse. The odds are better with a good rider on a good horse, but the greatest success comes when horse and rider, regardless of individual talents, are mentally and physically in sync. Their communication seems invisible, and trust is evident, making the ride flow smoothly and effortlessly.

The rider's style must meld with the horse's personality, and the rider must find a way to communicate nonverbally in a manner the horse understands and accepts. By "getting into the horse's mind," thinking like him, figuring the reasons behind his actions, and effectively communicating with him, the rider finds that the horse becomes eager to perform for him or her. Women, with our intuitive nature, are good at sensing what a horse feels and desires. The tendency for women to take cues from physical reactions and act with sensitivity and finesse help us train and relate to our horses.

Partly due to our physical limitations, women tend to find alternative, nonthreatening methods of accomplishing a task. Nurturing the horse in ways that are gentle, methodical, and patient, yet demand respect, often brings positive results. It may take repe-

tition and imagination, but persistence usually wins out. Strength, size, and power, attributes that enable men to dominate other sports, are less relevant in horse sports. The rider must have athletic ability, a competitive attitude, and good coordination, but sheer muscle power rarely comes into play. It is physically impossible to overpower a horse, and attempts to do so often bring resentment and ill will. I have seen few horses born with a stubborn and hateful attitude. Most are made so by misuse and abuse.

Each horse is an individual. Some are hot tempered, some calm. Some are brave, some fearful. Some seem to know the game and desire to win, while others would be content never to see the show ring. Trainers must be sensitive to each horse's needs. By trying to understand the way he thinks and by reading his reactions, we can adapt our methods of communication and training to build the horse's strength and confidence, thus enabling him to perform better.

Riding is not your typical sport; it requires dedication, persistence, and sacrifice. Yet it also brings tremendous rewards. Because riding relies more heavily on the relationship between horse and rider than on athletic power, it is a natural choice for women. It is one of the few sports in which men and women compete on an equal basis. The numerous women at the top continually prove one does not need a man's strength to succeed. It is a game of skill, agility, wit, athleticism, and most importantly, trust between partners. It is a team sport in which women are naturally suited to play an integral role in all parts of the support structure, be it as groom, vet, trainer, or rider. I think my attraction to horses (and that of most women's) can best be described as a passion for horses and for working with them. I feel lucky to be able to have a career with these wonderful animals.

lesley harrison
© 1992

# UNFINISHED BUSINESS

*by Melissa Holbrook Pierson*

*I hear the Shadowy Horses,*
*their long manes a-shake,*
*Their hoofs heavy with tumult,*
*their eyes glimmering white…*

—William Butler Yeats (1865–1939),
"He Bids His Beloved Be at Peace"

*As long as* I have been alive, it seems, I have wanted a horse. I still want a horse. It seems impossible that I will ever have one, even though I can look out my side window and see horses in the fields next door, even though I have a barn that needs only a new floor to house them and a pasture that needs only a brush hog and a fence to suit them. Lately, all the new friends I make seem to be members of what is to me the ultimate secret club: The Horsewomen. They must have a special handshake. They can no doubt identify each other through certain aspects of their appearances, then they repair into the warmth of the heated tack room to speak their language in code. I begin to wonder if horses, for me, have existed only to make me understand what the true nature of longing is.

The girl's powerful desire for the horse is undeniable but ultimately inexplicable, I've decided. It is a force as unchangeable as the weather. I can in some ways still feel it, but only in the way of a memory from long ago. It's like watching an old home movie of myself. I'm aware that I once was that small person up on the screen, and I may even recall the temperature on that day, the feel of the sun on my face, and what it was that had made me laugh. But I am struck, too, by a touch of sadness with the knowledge that I can never fully inhabit that child again. She is gone, taking with her the sense that the future is limitless. I see in the space of a single frame that the past is past, and I may never regain the absolute faith that I will have all the things I ever wanted, simply because I want them with such fire.

Each and every school horse, camp horse, livery horse I rode actually belonged to me—at least it did in that alternate universe I had constructed for us. It was a delicious place. I remember a palomino, a certain bay; I remember how everyone else would vanish when I buried my face in the horses' manes. No other girl was to possess these now nameless creatures because in the world of dreams, we had built a life together. That it was a fantasy did not make it insubstantial or misty. Hardly. Fantasy was the most solid thing there was, more so than the earth underfoot. It was where I truly lived, I and the horses who belonged to everyone but me.

By now I have learned too much, heard too much, and thought too much, all of which interfere with the production of simple dreams, the kind in which love is the only thing I need to spring lightly onto a bare back and canter off to the uncharted trail through the woods, knowing nothing bad will ever happen.

Perhaps what I miss most about those days when my longing was the driving force in my child-

ish life is the absence of any fear or uncertainty: *I was going to have a horse, and nothing could stop me.* Now, though I may seek to brush it away sometimes, fear and uncertainty always press their hot breath against my neck. The years between then and now have changed something in me, so that I listen to stories of what women do with their horses with a mixture of so many emotions it is almost scary. *Do you really think you would be able to do that? Could you possibly learn now all the things you would need to know to stay safe, to be humane, to forge a relationship with a one thousand–pound prey animal who speaks with his body?* The longing is now not so pure. Not so innocent. Not so ignorant.

As I return to the image of me as a little girl, I recall that I was once a member of that secret club, taking a bus home an hour and a half from Red Raider Camp every weekend, tired, dusty, redolent of pony, frayed crop sticking up from boot, with the girls on either side chattering happily of their exploits on horseback that wonderful day.

Wait—that was me? Then I must have also been the one who borrowed *every single book* the library had on the subject of horses, so it is possible that I do know a little more than I think. Perhaps there is a key to unlocking these facts, and all the other memories that seem lost, so that they will all come tumbling out to lie at my feet, as vibrant as on the day they were put away. Perhaps the key is the horse himself.

I can start to save my money. In the spring I will call the tractor man with the brush hog and the barn restorer. And then I will see if I really do long differently now than I did forty years ago, and if I can close the gap of decades, just like that, with a fantasy that becomes real, animated by a sweet breath that smells peculiarly like promise.

# BETTER RIDERS, BETTER MOTHERS

## by *Anna Jane White-Mullin*

*The spirited horse,*
*which will of itself strive to win the race,*
*will run still more swiftly if encouraged.*

—Ovid (43 BC–AD 18),
*Epistoloe Ex Ponto*

*I have often* thought that training a horse is excellent preparation for motherhood. It constantly requires both kindness and self-sacrifice. At the end of a long day of showing, for instance, a horse must be cooled down and have its legs wrapped before the rider treats herself to dinner and a bath. The young girl's willingness to put her horse first is no different from a mother's willingness to put her child first.

Horses and infants are constantly communicating with body language, and an astute female is able to interpret these signs and respond in an appropriate way. I often tell riding students to be "global learners," to keenly observe everything around them when they are dealing with a horse. A "visual learner" knows what she observes mostly through sight, and an "auditory learner" learns mostly by means of what she hears. But a global learner soaks up everything going on around her, such as the sound of the restless horse walking circles in a stall, the expression of tension in the horse's head and neck, or the feel of sweat as it breaks underneath the horse's coat. The global learner combines what her coach has said with what she has experienced for herself and comes to comprehensive conclusions about the horse. Is this not the same as the young mother who has watched her child become sick at home, made mental notes of everything that could come into play (such as temperature, eating habits, and sleeping habits), then headed to the doctor in search of a professional, medical opinion, using every resource to come to the correct conclusion?

Beyond kindness, self-sacrifice, and the ability to interpret body language, there is another important component that is shared between training horses and raising children: discipline. Whether with horse or child, discipline is successful only when it is consistent and meted out in an appropriate degree. The rule of thumb regarding horsemanship is to do only what it takes to get what you want. For example, if the horse will not go forward in response to the squeezing of the rider's legs, then the rider may add a little spur pressure or tap the horse on the flank with her stick if she is not wearing spurs. This is appropriate in degree for the horse's transgression of being unwilling to go forward from the leg. If the light use of the spur or stick gets the desired reaction—that is, the horse moves forward—then the degree of discipline is appropriate. If this does not get the desired effect, then the rider should increase the pressure of the aids incrementally, rather than going from light pressure to tremendous pressure. Had the rider initially responded with a painful blow of the whip on the horse's flank, then the horse would certainly go forward, but the degree of discipline would have been inappropriate, breaching the bond of trust that should always exist between a horse and a rider. This is similar to the bond of trust between mother and child, for the child should respect the mother but not fear her.

Consistency in discipline is another part of this equation. The happiest horses and children are those who know the rules and understand the consequences of breaking them. It takes constant effort as both a rider and a mother to make rules clear and enforce them in an appropriate manner. There should be rewards for good behavior and boundaries preventing bad behavior. For example, to prevent a horse from bolting out of the arena gate, the rider should always go past the opening, then circle back to exit. This action creates a boundary to prevent bad behavior. Once the horse has circled back and is quietly exiting the arena, the rider can reward the good behavior with a looser rein and a pat on the neck.

What we learn as riders should make us better mothers. We must always establish boundaries that encourage our children to do the right thing, then reward them when they do it. It can be as simple as saying, "Be sure to be home by 10:00 p.m.," then verbally rewarding them when they come home on time. You can say something such as, "You're such a responsible person. I know some parents have trouble with their children observing curfews, and I'm so glad I can trust you." Then, when the child asks to stay out a little later for some special event, you can say yes and again take the opportunity to mention how this privilege is based on the trust you've established through the child's previous good behavior.

Trust is everything. For a horse, it is being bathed in water that is a comfortable temperature, fed on time, or blanketed when the weather is cold. When trust is well established, you can get the very best from your horse—not only in a competitive setting, but also in other circumstances. A trusting horse is not difficult to groom or tack up and may even fall asleep while being bathed. A distrusting horse will constantly move around, staying overly alert while being groomed and tacked up.

For all the talking we humans do, the horse understands very little of it other than the sound of its own name and the tone of voice the person is using. The major means of communication, then, is touch. A big slap on the neck does not mean "good job old buddy," as some riders seem to think, but rather is just a big slap on the neck. It is only when the touch is comfortable and pleasing that the horse responds in a positive, trusting way.

Another means of establishing trust is by being empathetic to the horse's physical and mental state during exercise. Some riders work their horses for an extended period of time without a break, oblivious to the horse's discomfort and sometimes even pain. Working too long in a collected frame on the flat is torturous to a horse because it is unnatural for the animal's neck muscles. Bad riding on the flat in which the horse's head is behind the vertical plane and the rider is seesawing the chin back to the chest is especially painful for the horse and is an enormous breach of trust. The horse should get a break on a loose rein for at least a couple of minutes after every five minutes of flatwork. If you're working your horse on the flat and all is going well, then after a while, the animal begins to fight you, there's a good chance you made the mistake of working the horse too long without a break. Your horse is speaking to you with body language. If you can't interpret that language and inadvertently continue to keep your horse in an uncomfortable position, then the horse will eventually stop trusting you altogether.

For a child it is much the same—being kept clean, well fed, warm in the winter, and touched by a kind and loving hand establishes trust. Being forced to do something that is physically uncomfortable or mentally unsettling reduces the level of trust. In both horse and child, it is difficult to reestablish a high level of trust once it has been diminished.

Much of my work these days is devoted to reestablishing trust in horses. It is a slow process that requires empathy and patience, which when added to kindness, self-sacrifice, interpreting body language, disciplining in an appropriate and consistent way, setting boundaries for bad behavior, and estab-

lishing rewards for good behavior, can provide a broad-based road map to successful living. When I think of how much I love horses, I think of everything my experience with them has given me that has made me a better person—especially a better mother—than I might have been.

I think women have a natural bond with horses because women have been caregivers for centuries. It is not such a leap of the imagination that we who have traditionally responded in kindness and understanding to the speechless cries of an infant can innately perceive the silent needs of the horse. May we never lose sight of the intrinsic value of this primal gift.

*Anna Jane has made some keen observations about* the parallels between horse care and child rearing. Every year I teach twenty to thirty horse-training courses. In nearly every course, I've been asked the same question, "Can I use these same techniques to raise my children?" My answer is always the same, "Absolutely yes, the principles are the same."

To be a great horse teacher you must follow a few simple foundational rules:

- Yes means yes, and no means no

- There is black, white, and very little gray

- Reward every minute effort

- Be aggressive without being angry

- It takes as long as it takes

- Because I'm the alpha

- Consistency is everything

These are the rules that I have used to teach thousands of people about horses. When I teach them, I have no intentions of subliminally teaching parenting skills, but the list would probably provide a new parent with a pretty good foundation. I have raised two children. As of this writing, they are seventeen and nineteen years old. If I had to grade myself, I would guess that I earned a B- in parenting, and we managed to avoid all of the societal and behavioral traps that befall a good number of American teenagers. I tried to follow some basic principles with my kids that I also try to follow with horses. I don't think that these principles are ingenious or revolutionary, but they require time. Time is the one thing that lacks in most of my students' training routines. Unfortunately, time is also the one thing that is most lacking in the parent-child relationships that I am exposed to.

When working with horses, there is no way to substitute for the time spent teaching and learning. If a student does not have a certain amount of time that she can consistently devote to her horse, she will not see the kinds of results that she is hoping for. There are no quick fixes, there are no magic exercises, and without changing priorities, there are no unexpected results. The fact remains that what we care about most receives the most of our time.

So we read in magazines that your time is more valuable to your child than the things that you buy her. We justify time away from our children by claiming that "the private school education" is worth the sacrifice. We think "the nice neighborhood with nice children" or "having a room of her own" is more important than spending hours communicating with our kids. But we are wrong. There is nothing more important to a child's development, education, and foundation than spending time with her parents.

Without time, you cannot have a meaningful relationship with your horse. Without that relationship, you cannot expect to be taken seriously when you attempt to teach or guide your horse. Without your teaching or guidance, your horse doesn't need you for anything more than food, clothing, and shelter—and neither does your child.

# COMMUNICATING WITH MY HORSE

*by Kathy Hawkins*

*You and your horse. His strength and beauty.
Your knowledge and patience and
determination and understanding and love.
That's what fuses the two of you into this marvelous
partnership that makes you wonder…
"What can heaven offer any better than
what I have here on earth?"*

—Monica Dickens (1915–1992), English writer

To start this story, I have to thank my parents, Larry and Carolyn Hawkins, for letting me pursue my love and passion for horses. My parents were not horse people, so they didn't have the same passion or love for horses that I have. But if it weren't for them, I would never have had the chance to follow my dreams. For thirty-three years now I have been working with horses. I have learned a lot over the years but still learn a little more every day.

My love for horses began at an early age. I started English riding lessons when I was seven, with a lot of bumps and bruises, and I continued lessons for several years. Then I was able to ride and to somewhat train horses for other people. At age eighteen, I was able to purchase my first horse, which was a real dream come true. Of course the horse I purchased was a mare and she was pregnant. So soon I was raising my first foal. What a joy it was to learn from a young one. It was then that I learned how a mare communicates, teaches, and disciplines her little one. I took those methods to heart and began to use them in my training techniques.

Have you ever just sat and watched a herd of horses, watched to see who the leader is and which one is at the bottom of the pecking order? When a herd comes to a watering hole or trough, the leader drinks first, the others wait their turn in order. Seeing behaviors like this teaches us about how horses communicate with each other. Not that I am a great trainer or even profess to be, but I found that it is important to learn to communicate with a horse—to think like the horse does. We must learn how horses communicate so we can gain their respect. We must gain respect to be the leader of the herd; we have to be that alpha mare. In my training techniques, I expect respect from my horses and they

know it. I am the leader of the herd, even though that authority will be challenged from time to time.

As long as you expect respect from them, foals will begin to understand that you, the handler, are now the alpha mare. If you let them run over you and push you around, then you have not fully gained their respect. I am not talking about them wanting you to love them; I am talking about them biting at you, turning hindquarters to you in a threatening manner, laying their ears back at you, not accepting you as the leader. This is pure disrespect, and you should not allow it from any horse no matter what the age. Like I said, all horses will challenge you at one time or another, so you have to stay consistent and remain the leader.

From the time a foal is born here, he or she is imprinted to gain knowledge for the future. The foal learns to bond with people, to be touched and

controlled by people without being afraid. Time and time again, as the foal is growing, I remind him or her of what had been learned before. When the time comes for the foal to be weaned, a new bond has formed between the foal and me. By the age of two, these horses will be more trusting, and they will be calm and eager to please.

I do not use fear in my training methods; to gain respect does not mean a horse has to be treated in a harsh way. I use a reward and discipline method. When I ask my horse a question and he answers correctly, he gets a reward. I'm not saying he gets a cookie, but he may get to rest for a minute or even have the pressure released from his mouth—simple little rewards mean a lot. If my horse has to work a little harder to answer correctly, I don't whip it into him. I patiently give him time, and I think about whether I am asking in a way he can understand. I consider how my horse is responding to the question. If he is acting totally confused and trying to do something different from what I am asking, I try asking the question in a simpler form. I watch for even the smallest effort, reward that effort, and then require a little more from him the next time. As long as he knows what I'm asking, he will be happy to answer the question.

Getting back to women and horses, I think that a woman and a horse have the same type of relationship as a mare and a foal; both pairs show the love, compassion, and respect they feel for one another. A woman or girl, I feel, has a greater sense of the love and compassion—the need to touch, feel, and caress as a mother does her child—than a man or boy does. I believe that horses can sense this in a woman. I feel that women are much more patient than men are with their horses.

Women get frustrated too, but it is easier for us to take a step back, look at the situation, and find a better solution. How often do you see a male trainer gouging the side of his horse with spurs to get the response he wants? I'm not talking about just touching the horse with spurs, I mean digging the spurs in. I am certainly not against using spurs, but I feel they should be used in the correct manner, not as a punishing tool. Just take a spur and gouge your side a few times; that is what your horse feels. Hurts, don't it? I'm not saying all men are, but some are a little rougher than women are. That is just my thought for the day.

What would happen if we didn't teach the generations after us how to love and treat horses? Would these lessons just get abandoned and go by the wayside? Would anyone care? I feel that we must teach our children to be responsible for these majestic creatures given to us by God, our father. So spend time with your child to enjoy her while she is young. Take the chance; let your child experience horses. Ride with her; teach her all that you know about how to care for horses. Sending a child for riding lessons, as my parents did for me, may be the greatest thing you could ever do. Let your child find out if horses are her passion; if they are, she can carry this passion with her in life. Then when she has children of her own, maybe she will do the same for them.

I think God's gift to women is the horse. He wants us to have pleasurable things; I think that is why He gave us animals to care for and to be our companions. He didn't give horses voices, but He did give them the ability to feel unconditional love for us. We can spread our wings and enjoy nature with these majestic creatures. Horses allow us to be independent and to have the freedom to express our love.

# AUTHOR,
# LIFE-LONG EQUESTRIAN

*by Cali Canberra*

*The best cure in the world for writer's block*
*is a canter through the woods.*

—Cooky McClung, "First Things First" in
*The Chronicle of the Horse*

*I can't help* comparing my own life to that of my horses. They live on seventy-five acres of pastureland with an abundance of trees for shelter and a clear running stream. I live in a subdivision on less than a half an acre, and I don't have much of a view. As in a true herd environment, my horses live with thirty others. I have one human friend. My horses receive the best nutrition, health care, barefoot trimming, grooming, and handling that time, love, and money can allow. I don't always eat the healthy food I should, I get my hair cut at a discount chain rather than at a salon, and I've never had a manicure or a pedicure. My horses have had more chiropractic adjustments than I have, and they've had more massages than I have (I do their massages). I stretch them, but I don't always stretch myself after strenuous exercise. I energy balance my horses more often than I balance myself. I show them compassion and affection, and reward them for their willingness to please me. I wish I was one of my horses.

In return, my horses keep me sane. They keep me functioning when I experience turbulent personal and business times, and trail riding inspires my creativity. I write novels about the horse business, and I work out my plots and character motivations when I ride—my mind is clear and the fresh air relaxes me. My horses satisfy my need for a close relationship outside my family. I can trust them to be accessible whenever I need them and not to betray me. They aren't judgmental, critical, or opinionated. They ask very little of me. Horses don't lie, cheat, or steal. They're honest—if you allow them to be. I have learned more from horses than I have from any person, book, or educational opportunity.

I depend on my horses more than they depend on me. They're fond of me: they come running when I call them, and when I turn them back out after a ride or just a feeding and grooming, they voluntarily stay next to me until I walk away first. They have all the necessities in life without me (assuming you think horses can live without fly and worm control, vaccines, and hoof trimming), and I know they don't really need me emotionally.

My horses know I'm their leader at all times, without exception. We have a mutual respect that can be relied on. I consistently communicate with them both intuitively and through clear and precise signals so they don't become confused. They always know their place, and I know mine. I must think like a horse since a horse can't learn to think like a person. With patience, perseverance, gentle

guidance, and a reward system, my horses have learned that I'm not the enemy, I'm their protector and friend; I hold the alpha position. They know I will not use force or intimidate or do anything that causes them physical pain. Because I allow them to communicate with me, they are willing partners. We enjoy a relationship closer than most people imagine a horse and owner can have. My horses rarely refuse anything because I allow them time to learn, absorb, and accept a situation, never pushing too hard before they are emotionally and physically ready.

My horses know they can't take advantage of me, but of course, they're not perfect all of the time. When I need to, I'll use a progressing amount of firmness, depending upon their reaction. If a horse acts up for no good reason, I first use my voice. If the response is not what I want, I raise my crop toward his shoulder (I ride with a crop to ward off pesky insects I can't reach) and usually that's the most I need to do. On occasion, I need to give a firm thump from the crop on the rear end or on the shoulder, which definitely works unless there is something extremely important my horse is warning me about. That's completely different!

I trust my horses' instincts. I don't spoil them, but I listen to them, which gives us a relationship of trust. For example, if Cabaret were to stop walking and look toward a thicket of trees, perk his ears, and raise his head, I would allow him to stop. He knows I won't force him to go where he is concerned there may be danger. Instead, I let him see that there are no monsters behind the trees. If I just wait a moment with my relaxed seat and take a few deep breaths that gently radiate through my body and into his, he'll take my cue and move on.

After his basic training was completed, it turned out that the only time Cabaret didn't move on cue, his instinct was correct. We were heading toward a water crossing. When we approached the immediate area, he stopped in his tracks. When he didn't respond to my progressively firm cues for him to continue on, I trusted him, dismounted, and led him toward the water. The area had collapsed and there was now a shear drop. Cabaret looked at me as if to say, "See, I told you we shouldn't go there!"

Horses seek freedom along with guidance. I like to give my horses choices every once in a while during a ride. On one out of every seven or eight rides, I let my horses tell me where they want to go and at what speed they want to move. I learn about them, what they want to see, their moods, and their physical states. I think this lets them know I just want to be with them and am curious about what they are interested in. They never take advantage of me when I give them this freedom. As soon as I decide to be in control again, they follow my guidance without any resistance.

I understand my horses in every way humanly possible. I know what's normal for my horses because I pay attention to the way they carry themselves, the brightness in their eyes, their alertness and energy levels and overall attitude. I study their demeanor, watch to see if they are cocking a leg more frequently than usual, and pay attention to whether they are bearing an even amount of weight on all four legs the majority of the time. I can tell if their facial expressions change, which may indicate pain or that healing has finally occurred. I believe that if you care about your horse's physical well-being as much as his psychological well-being (and you know what to look for),

your relationship will be enhanced, therefore enhancing the rewards and pleasures of being with that horse, even if you don't own him. I treat horses the way they deserve to be treated and the way that I wish people would treat each other: with compassion, consideration, and respect.

One of my most rewarding experiences with horses is when I can heal them physically and emotionally. Over the years, I've learned about yin and yang, acupuncture, acupressure, chiropractic, therapeutic massage, and Linda Tellington-Jones's Healing Touch System. They all have one thing in common: energy forces. The world and all living things are about energy. I learned about "life-force" energy, known as chi. There are specific areas on the body where the chi can be accessed to energetically stimulate all vital parts of the body. By stimulating these areas, energy blocks and energy imbalances can be corrected, and health can be restored. This method heals horses physically and emotionally without having to inflict pain.

As an example, I owned a breeding stallion who was always full of tension during breeding season: his muscles were constantly tensed, and he was always pacing in his pasture, looking for mares who might be in season. In his stall, he was always on high alert, never relaxed. One night, when I was up waiting for a mare to foal, I decided to do an energy balancing on my stallion. Within fifteen minutes, my stallion completely relaxed, his muscles softened, his head hung low, and he licked his lips. Then he collapsed in his stall! At first I panicked. Then after I regained my composure, I let him remain lying in his thick shavings. I finished the energy balancing, and then closed his energetic

pathways. Within a few minutes, my stallion stood, shook himself off, and remained relaxed and content for at least two weeks. Apparently, I had released his pent-up energy. After that, every time he became tense, I balanced him and he was fine. He never collapsed again because there wasn't enough build-up to cause such a strong release. Keep in mind, I never physically touched the horse throughout the entire process.

I have so many stories like this. In the past several years, I've cured dozens of my own horses' colic episodes and those of horses at the barn where I now board. I don't believe that I have a special gift or power to heal. I believe that anyone who wants to learn how to do it, and who is genuinely open to the idea, can do the same. Equally important to physically healing a horse is fixing emotional problems and breaking down certain fears. This, too, can

be done using energy manipulation techniques. Because women are generally more patient than men, we are more likely to be successful.

I believe that every moment I'm with my horses, we're teaching each other something. Some days I'm teaching them only that they can count on me to be there, and some days the lessons are more complex, like working on backing up in a circle or side passing down a fence line. Every day I have with my horses is a rewarding experience for me regardless of what we've done. Often, it's the simplest accomplishments that bring me the most pleasure.

I've accepted full responsibility as a horse owner to improve their lives and my own. Through horses, I've learned so many lessons, including how to be free-spirited and tranquil. Like many women with horses, I can't imagine living without these magnificent creatures in my life.

# DREAMS DO COME TRUE

## by Rachel Allgyer

*[The mare] set off for home with the speed of a swallow,*
*and going as smoothly and silently.*
*I never had dreamed of such a motion,*
*fluent and graceful, and ambient,*
*soft as the breeze flitting over the flowers,*
*but swift as the summer lightning.*

—Richard Doddridge Blackmore (1825–1900),
English writer

# Horses amaze me.

I've grown up with them, interacted with them since I was a toddler, yet the awe I've always felt only becomes deeper. I grew up in an Amish family, where we use some of our horses for transportation and work. So by depending on horses the way we do, and also since my family (especially Dad) loves horses, I learned early in my life how wonderful they are. Every day after school I would run to the barn or to one of the pastures just to make sure the horses were all okay or to bring apples to them. As they started running to meet me and nickering in greeting, my heart would be completely lost to them.

When I was a teenager, a black foal, who I absolutely loved, was born on our farm. He was the prettiest colt you ever saw (at least I thought so). Even though I didn't know if Dad would sell him or which trainer he would be sent to, I let myself dream.

I sat under the tree in the pasture and wondered what if I could somehow train him someday? What if we could grow to trust each other so much that we could be as one and do anything together? As I sat there dreaming and watching him run alongside his mother, I pictured myself riding across the fields on the back of this beautiful black horse, needing only the lightest of cues between us to communicate.

Most of all, I wanted the horse and me to learn together. I didn't want a trainer, who would probably never see him again, to form that relationship with my horse. I wanted to be a team with him. But since I didn't know anybody who trained horses, and I had no idea how to begin training, it seemed like an unreachable dream.

A couple of months later, my dad took me to the Maryland Horse Expo, and I met the person who played the biggest part in making my dream

185

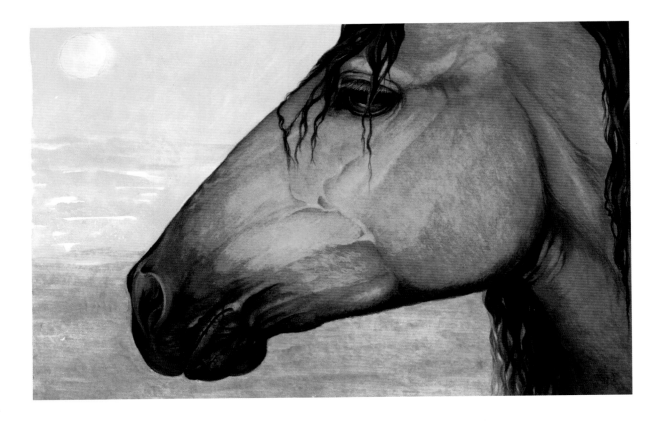

come true. I sat in the bleachers that day, watching Pony Boy and thinking there is someone who really, truly, understands horses. That must have been one of the most amazing hours of my life—realizing that the connection I felt with horses could take me as far as I'd ever dreamed. Suddenly my unreachable dream was within my reach.

By attending Pony's clinics at expos and by reading his books, I learned how to communicate effectively with my horse. Through hours and hours of working with the beautiful black foal now named Black Powder, the two of us developed a relationship even beyond what I had ever imagined. And as the two of us kept learning together, naturally, Black Powder became my horse. No one would ever dream of separating us.

Sometimes I wonder why something as simple as sitting on a fence as the sun sets, watching the horses quietly graze gives me such a peaceful feeling. Why, when on the back of my horse running with the wind, do I feel such wonder? And why do I feel the thrill run straight to my toes when the horses see me at the gate, leave their grazing, and start galloping toward me?

I've learned so much from horses. I've reached my dream of communicating with and training horses. I think the bond between women and horses is a gift from God; He wanted to show in one more way what an amazing God He is. I hope we never take for granted the gift we have in horses. And always, follow your dreams—all the way! Nothing is impossible!

*Reading Rachel's essay brings a smile to my face and* a tear to my eye. Although she is my son's age and was brought up in an entirely different cultural surrounding, she and I are kindred. When I see her interact with, learn about, and watch horses, I recognize the knowing that is in her eyes. I recently had the opportunity to see a side of a horsewoman that I have never seen before.

I met Rachel and her brother at the horse expo in Maryland and shortly thereafter had the pleasure of meeting her dad at a farm auction in Lancaster County, Pennsylvania. Since our families became friends, kids with kids and adults with adults, we have become quite a motley crew. I count this family among my closest friends.

Over the years we have vacationed together, attended church together, played Monopoly until the wee hours of the night, and turned more than a few heads at places like Outback Steakhouse and Applebee's. If you should ever be out to dinner and notice an Indian guy, his family, and fourteen to twenty Amish folks—that's us. Come on over and say hello.

The horse Rachel writes about in her essay is Black Powder. After learning of his daughter's longing for the foal, her dad gave Black Powder to Rachel. She beamed for months. Her dad bought her a round pen, a saddle, and anything else that she needed to train her horse. Watching Rachel in the round pen was not much different from watching one of my training videos. She has the "feel," and her horse knew it.

I got a call not so long ago that Black Powder had to be taken to the veterinary school for bad colic. I was in the Canary Islands at the time and did the only thing that I could. I prayed. I prayed that if Black Powder did not make it, Rachel's broken heart would not prevent her from pursuing her dreams. Several days later, I received the news that Black Powder had died. My wife and I sent flowers and said a prayer for Rachel.

I have been around horses for a long time. I have seen many horses sicken and I have seen too many die from colic. Several months after Black Powder's death, I was reminded of what it means to lose your best equine friend. We were visiting for the holidays, and my wife and I were staying in Rachel's room. At the foot of the bed lay a tribute to her best friend and teacher. The display included a piece of his tail, braided and tied, his breed registry papers, photos of Black Powder, the flowers that we and many others had sent, cards, letters, and many, many candles, both burning and spent.

I have never seen a more sincere exhibit of a person's feelings for a horse. The entire room overflowed with gratitude for what she had learned from him and what he had given her. No horse has ever had a better friend than Black Powder had in Rachel.

# Biographies

### RACHEL ALLGYER

Growing up in the heart of Pennsylvania Dutch Country, in an Amish family, Rachel Allgyer has been surrounded by horses since birth. After meeting GaWaNi Pony Boy and attending his clinics, Rachel was able to realize her dream of learning to effectively communicate with and train her horse Black Powder.

### GEORGINA BLOOMBERG

Born and raised in New York City, Georgina Bloomberg has been riding since age four. She began competing in the pony ranks and, as a junior rider and jumper, garnered numerous championships and honors. As a young adult, she has become a grand prix winner in horse show jumping and in April 2005, at age twenty-two, became the youngest rider ever to qualify for the FEI World Cup Finals.

### KAREN BRENNER

Karen Brenner's equine paintings capture everyday moments in the lives of horses. The favorite part of each project for Karen is the time spent quietly observing her subject. Karen enjoys trail riding with her husband and their three Quarter Horses, as well as training her Andalusian filly. A member of the Equine Artists Guild and the Ohio Horsemen's Council, Karen received a BFA from Miami University. She lives in Wooster, Ohio.

### CALI CANBERRA

Cali Canberra has spent her life with horses: riding, training, breeding, brokering, and selling Arabians, Quarter Horses, and Thoroughbreds. Through Alt Creations, Cali designs and markets her line of equestrian-imaged stationary, note cards, and other gift items. Though no longer working in the horse industry, she writes fiction about the inner workings of the horse business. She is the author of *Trading Paper, Never Enough!* and *Buying Time*.

### LAURA CHAPOT

Daughter of U.S. Olympic show-jumping riders Mary and Frank Chapot, Laura Chapot grew up surrounded by horses and progressed through the equine ranks from ponies, equitation, and hunters to show jumpers. A championship rider, Laura has won numerous national and international competitions and represented the United States Equestrian Team.

### LISA COLOMBE

Currently director of Sinte Gleska University Ranch, Lisa Colombe has developed a groundbreaking approach to providing access for tribal members to tribal lands through the reintroduction of horses into Lakota culture. With programs now extending in to the Natural Resources and Animal Science, Lisa continues to be fundamental in the university's growth and expansion. She also enjoys breakaway roping and barrel racing and has been competing professionally for the past three years.

## PEGGY CUMMINGS

Peggy Cummings, who grew up in San Salvador, has a gift for translating classical riding principles through techniques that allow horses and riders to move with freedom of movement instead of bracing and tension. Riding masters such as Sally Swift, Linda Tellington-Jones, and Anders Lindgren were influential in shaping the unique riding and training method Peggy now calls Connected Riding. She travels internationally, giving demonstrations, clinics, and seminars.

## DEBBIE DOLAN-SWEENEY

During her career, Debbie Dolan-Sweeney has had numerous Grand Prix wins. Other notable achievements include being the first American rider to win the prestigious British Ladies Show Jumping Championship in Windsor, England. She has been a member of winning USET Nations' Cup Teams in international competitions.

## LILIANA GOMEZ

Liliana Gomez has shown extensively in her native Bogota, Colombia. Known for her unique and passionate depiction of horses, she has also displayed great talent in expressing her love of people. Now a Canadian resident, she has embraced her new culture, while capturing her heritage, in her latest collection, *Colombian Children . . . and Horses.*

## JULIE GOODNIGHT

An equine professional for more than twenty years, with a background ranging from dressage and jumping to racing, reining, colt-starting, and wilderness riding, Julie Goodnight is known for her upbeat, logical teaching style and ability to bridge natural horsemanship techniques with the principles of classical riding. Owner of Goodnight Training Stables, Inc., she spends much of the year traveling the country conducting horsemanship clinics.

## HEIDI HARNER

Heidi Harner is a watercolor artist in Indiana whose art centers on painting horses and pet portraits. Her graphic design training from Purdue University enhances the design, color, and composition in her paintings. Her resident artist position at the Museum at Prophetstown allows her to observe and appreciate Belgian horses. Heidi and husband Brad share their home with his daughter and two dogs.

## CAROL HARRIS

Carol Harris owns Bo-Bett Farm, in Reddick, Florida, which has produced many top halter, performance, and racehorses. Carol was an American Quarter Horse judge for many years, pioneering the way for other women. After moving to Florida in 1963, she dedicated herself to the Florida Quarter Horse Association, becoming president for three consecutive terms. In 1997, the AQHA inducted her into their hall of fame, recognizing her contributions to the American Quarter Horse.

## LESLIE HARRISON

Very few artists achieve Lesley's Harrison's level of technical excellence. Even fewer capture the spirit, the emotion, and the lifelike realism for which

Lesley's work is known. One of the finest U.S. pastel artists, Lesley chooses her subjects primarily for the emotion they evoke in her, hoping to convey those same feeling to others through her art.

## KATHY ANN HAWKINS

Kathy Ann Hawkins and her husband established Rockin H Quarter Horses in 1997 and started breeding for a quality performance cow and all-around horse. When she is not working with the horses, she cares for people as a registered nurse. Getting away with her family and horses is one of her favorite relaxation activities.

## SHAWNA KARRASCH

Shawna Karrasch spent nearly ten years working to perfect her animal training skills at Sea World of California with marine mammals. Few Sea World visitors ever get to see the training process that builds trust between animal and trainer, unlocking the animal's desire to perform. Shawna brought this remarkable process to the equine world and now teaches horse enthusiasts and professionals alike to use The On Target Training system.

## ALEXANDRA LAYOS

A seventeen-year-old honor student at Allentown Central Catholic High School, Alexandra Layos became a junior editor for the international show horse magazine *Saddle & Bridle* at age ten writing monthly articles for them ever since. She has published two books, *The Missing Link*, the first in an equine fiction series, and *An Almost True Horse Tale*, a children's picture book. Allie credits her best friend, a Morgan named Astonishinglee, as her inspiration.

## SYLVIA LOCH

Sylvia Loch has been teaching the art of classical riding for well over three decades. She and her late husband Lord Loch were among the first people to use Lusitano and Spanish horses at their dressage academy, first in Portugal and later the UK. In 1982 they founded the Lusitano Breed Society of Great Britain. As a trainer, writer, and lecturer, Sylvia has become a household name in the world of dressage. Today, the majority of her teaching work takes her back to Portugal, where she trains at Don Francisco de Braganca's classical academy near Lisbon.

## KIM MCELROY

In creating her art, Kim McElroy looks beyond the physical part of the horse to the truth of his benevolent, spiritual nature. This unique ability enables her to express the horse's entire being rather than mere likeness. At times she portrays horses as ethereal spirits, symbolically blended with the forces of nature, while her more realistic portraits capture the emotional, spiritual, and dynamic presence of these magnificent creatures.

## MARGO MCKNIGHT

Nature photographer and painter Margo McKnight is a nationally renowned artist whose passion for horses began in early childhood. A concern for the natural world led to a career in zoology and conservation, including a six-year, highly successful tenure as director of Florida's Brevard Zoo.

## LOLA MICHELIN

Lola Michelin has more twenty-five years of experience in the veterinarian and zoological fields. In

2001, after several years of successful practice in massage for horses, dogs, and people, she founded the Northwest School of Animal Massage. She speaks and writes regularly on the topic of animal massage and has appeared on television and radio as an advocate for animal therapies.

### LINDA "CHIGGER" MILLER

Linda "Chigger" Miller resides in East Tennessee at the foot of the Great Smoky Mountains National Park. She is a respected rider, instructor, and stable owner, enjoys pleasure riding and raising horses, and has competed successfully in the show ring. She believes strongly that a good rider can train a good horse and a good horse can train a good rider.

### LYNN PALM

A professional horsewoman for more than three decades, Lynn Palm is a successful competitor, trainer, clinician, and author. She holds numerous U.S. European championships and is a regular commentator on Horse TV and RFD-TV and a regular contributor to equine publications. Through her Palm Partnership Training education schools and clinics, she champions the partnership of horse and rider.

### MELISSA HOLBROOK PIERSON

Melissa Holbrook Pierson is a writer who has always felt more akin to animals than to those of her own kind. She is the author of *Dark Horses and Black Beauties: Animals, Women, a Passion*, which the *Times* of London called "wayward and brilliant." She lives on a former horse farm in upstate New York.

### PAT ROBERTS

Pat Roberts has bred, trained, and exhibited numerous champion horses. She is an artist whose unique style of sculpture allows her to capture her favorite subject, the horse in motion, in a very realistic way, with just a touch of impressionism. Her sculpture is part of the permanent collection at the European Museum of Art. Pat has collectors in 13 countries, and her sculptures are among the royal family's collection in England.

### CHERI SORENSEN

Born and raised in central Iowa, Cheri remembers working as a trail guide and spending much of her free time with pencil in hand. A self-taught artist, she has accumulated several awards and honors, including winning the Kansas Wildlife Art Series, Duck's Unlimited Artist of the year for an Iowa Chapter, and Elk Breeders Association Artist of the Year. Her artwork has been featured in magazines and used for advertising equine products.

### KARMEL TIMMONS

Karmel Timmons entered drawings in competitions throughout her teens but did not become a professional artist until she moved to Elbert, Colorado, an extremely "horsy" community. There she found the subjects that she felt were worthy of the hundreds of hours her works require. She has exhibited her work extensively and won several awards.

### SARET TOLA

Saret Tola owns Jump Start Farm (Paso Robles, California), specializing in warmblood sporthorse breeding (hunter/jumper/dressage). Through her homebred horses who have been decorated with many national and regional prizes and awards, she has become one of the most highly regarded sporthorse breeders in the nation.

### DAWN TRINKLER

Dawn Trinkler is a University of Kansas graduate, with a major in fine art and minors in photography and illustration. Through her paintings, she seeks to share with the world the wondrous beauty and intimacy within horses. Dawn's work is a conversation of spiritual energy and personal encounter.

### KATIE UPTON

Katie Upton studied art at Santa Barbara City College and the University of California, Santa Barbara. Her art is currently displayed in galleries in California, Colorado, and Vermont and held in private collections throughout the United States, as well as in Europe and Asia. She is recognized primarily for her large-scale oil paintings.

### ANNA JANE WHITE-MULLIN

At age thirteen, Anna Jane White-Mullin began competing in large East Coast horse shows. In 1971, she won the Alfred B. Maclay Finals and received a gold medal for winning twenty USET classes. While pursuing a broadcasting career, she has kept her equestrian ties, giving riding clinics, judging shows, and lecturing throughout the United States. Her first book, *Judging Hunters and Hunter Seat Equitation* (1984), was a best-seller.

"THERE IS NOTHING MORE DIFFICULT FOR A TRULY CREATIVE PAINTER THAN TO PAINT A ROSE, BECAUSE BEFORE HE CAN DO SO HE HAS FIRST TO FORGET ALL THE ROSES THAT WERE EVER PAINTED."

HENRI MATISSE

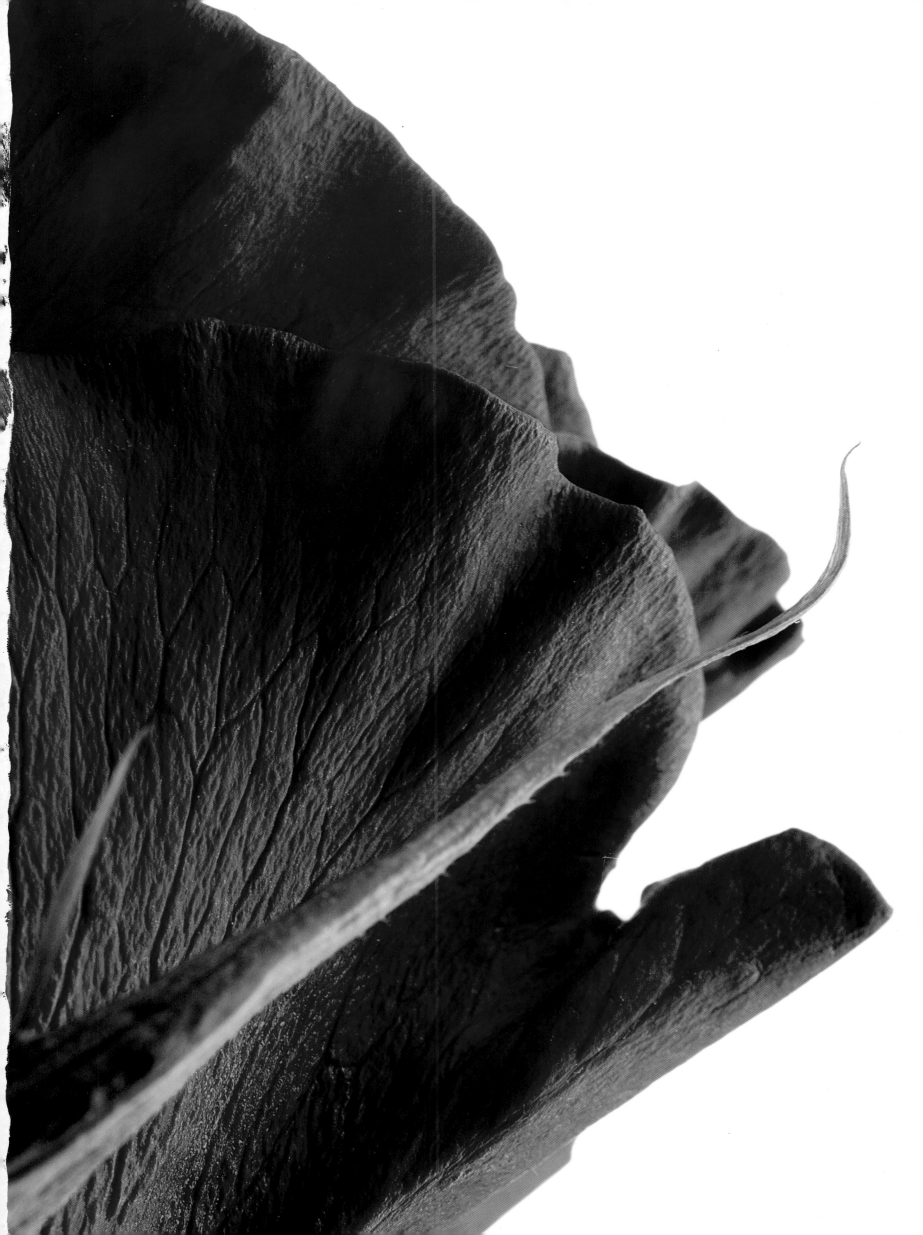

# ROSES

Photographs by *Fabio Petroni*

Text by *Natalia Fedeli*

**vmb**
PUBLISHERS

# "Contents"

Project editor  *Valeria Manferto De Fabianis*
Graphic design  *Marinella Debernardi*
Editorial staff  *Laura Accomazzo and Giorgio Ferrero*

THE WORLD OF FRESH CUT ROSES IS FASCINATING BUT ALSO COMPLICATED, MADE UP OF GROUPS, FAMILIES AND STRANGE RELATIONSHIPS. IT IS A WORLD IN WHICH MAN HAS OFTEN AND WILLINGLY DEALT BY PLAYING CUPID AND POINTING HIS BOW AND ARROWS TO CONCOCT FLORAL MARRIAGES WHICH WOULD NEVER EVER HAVE COME ABOUT NATURALLY. THE RESULT?

IT HAS BECOME A MULTI-ETHNIC PROGENY OF ROSES, AN EVER JUVENILE POPULATION IN MOVEMENT, GROWING IN NUMBER WITH NEW VARIETIES, BUT WHICH ALSO SEES THE DISAPPEARANCE OF OTHERS THAT ARE MORE SENSITIVE TO THE WHIMS OF THE GURUS OF FLORAL DÉCOR AND FASHION.

BUT WHY A BOOK ON FLORIST ROSES? SIMPLY BECAUSE THEY ARE SO BEAUTIFUL AND OFTEN ENTER OUR HOMES. THEY ARE THE FRUIT OF LONG, PATIENT AND ACCURATE WORK THAT RENDERS A TRIBUTE NOT ONLY TO BEAUTY BUT ALSO TO THE ABILITY OF MAN. THEIR PETALS ARE SILKY LIKE VELVET OR SUGAR, AND WITH LONG STEMS, GREEN HEART-SHAPED LEAVES, THEIR PALLET OF COLORS CAN RIVAL THE ALMOST INFINITE SHADES OF THE PANTONE COLOR MATCHING SYSTEM. WE SEE THESE ROSES IN FLOWER SHOPS, *GARDEN CENTERS*, AT MARKET STANDS AND AT IMPORTANT AND MEANINGFUL MOMENTS OF OUR LIVES. THEY NEVER FAIL TO BE PRESENT IN OUR DAILY ROUTINE.

THESE ROSES BOTANISTS CALL "HYBRID TEAS," ARE THE RESULT OF INFLEXIBLE AND CONSTANT RESEARCH WORK WHICH, FOR 150 YEARS, HAS SEEN MAN CHALLENGE HIMSELF AND NATURE, IN THE ATTEMPT TO CREATE THE "BEST" VARIETY, THE NEW, PRODUCTIVE, STRONG AND TODAY, THE MOST RESISTANT TO THE STRESS OF *JET LAGS*. IT HAS BEEN SO, THAT IN THE AGE OF GLOBALIZATION, ROSES GROWN NOT ONLY IN HOLLAND, FRANCE, ITALY, GERMANY, BUT ALSO IN ECUADOR, KENYA AND COLOMBIA, ARE SOLD ALL OVER THE WORLD. THE OPINION OF RENOWNED LANDSCAPIST AND PASSIONATE ITALIAN GARDEN DESIGNER, MAURIZIO USAI, ON THE HYBRID TEAS IS THAT, "THEY ARE A VERY IMPORTANT GROUP. ON ONE HAND THEY GAVE RISE TO THE MARKET OF FLORIST ROSES, AND ON THE OTHER HAVE DETERMINED THE BIRTH OF THE SO-CALLED MODERN ROSES."

THESE PAGES PRESENT A SELECTION OF SOME OF THE MOST REPRESENTATIVE AND INTERESTING TYPES OF FLORIST ROSES. FABIO PETRONI, MASTER OF *STILL LIFE* PHOTOGRAPHY, HAS MANAGED TO SUCCESSFULLY MERGE HIS PROFESSION WITH PASSION FOR NATURE, AND WAS ABLE TO CAPTURE THROUGH HIS LENS AND PARTICULAR SEN-

SITIVITY, ASPECTS AND DETAILS THAT MAKE EACH FLOWER UNIQUE, HIGHLIGHTING ITS FEATURES, SECRETS AND EMOTIONS. IT IS EXACTLY THESE EMOTIONS THAT ROSES ARE ABLE TO AROUSE, THAT INSPIRED THE CHAPTERS OF THIS VOLUME, SINCE EACH PRESENTS A BOUQUET SPECIFICALLY CREATED BY AN ITALIAN FLOWER MASTER, LIKE MARGHERITA ANGELUCCI: A BOUQUET "OF THE SOUL," A "SUNSHINE" BOUQUET, ONE THAT COMES "FROM THE HEART." THE ETHEREAL AND EVASIVE SOUL CALLS TO MIND THE WHITE COLOR WHICH IN ROSES ASSUMES AN INFINITE SERIES OF SHADES THAT GO FROM PURE SNOW TO POWDERY CREAM, TO LEMON GREEN AND UP TO PINKISH BEIGE. THE ROSES THAT DRAW INSPIRATION FROM THE LIGHT OF THE SUN AND TO ITS MORE OR LESS INTENSE HUES DURING THE SPAN OF THE DAY, MAKE YELLOW THEIR MATRIX AND ON CANVAS EXHIBIT THEIR PETALS IN AN OVERWHELMING VARIETY OF HUES THAT SEEM TO HAVE COME FROM THE COLOR PALETTES OF GREAT ARTISTS. IN THIS FLORAL COLLECTION, WHAT COULD NOT BE LEFT OUT IS RED, OF THE HEART AND PASSION AND SENTIMENTS WHICH ARE ALWAYS EXPRESSED IN EVER NEW AND UNPREDICTABLE WAYS. FROM RUBY TO CRIMSON, MAUVE TO PINK, FUCHSIA TO LACQUER RED, EACH ROSE IS ABLE TO INTERPRET AND INCARNATE SENTIMENTS TO PERFECTION.

WHAT ARE THE HISTORY, ORIGIN AND CHARACTERISTICS OF THESE ROSES? FRUIT OF THE CROSSBREEDING BETWEEN A HYBRID PERPETUAL AND A TEA ROSE, THESE FLOWERS ARE VERY PARTICULAR. ABOVE ALL, THE PLANTS ARE VERY LUXURIANT AND PRODUCE STEMS THAT ARE UPRIGHT, STRONG AND WITH LENGTHS OF MORE THAN 100 CENTIMETERS PER FLOWER. THE HIGH-CENTERED BUD IS PUFFED, POINTED AND BLOOMS IN A BIG CUP-SHAPED COROLLA WITH LARGE PETALS, CONCAVED AND THINNED OUT TOWARDS THE CENTER.

TO CROSS-BREED MEANS TO CREATE NEW VARIETIES. THE STILL VERY EMPIRICAL PRACTICE TAKES AT LEAST FIVE YEARS OF WORK IN OPEN FIELDS OR GREENHOUSES, AND VARIOUS MANUAL OPERATIONS. A NEW ROSE IN FACT, IS CREATED THROUGH SEXUAL REPRODUCTION AND HUMAN INTERVENTION IS DECISIVE. DEBORAH GHIONE WHO WORKS WITH THE FRENCH HYBRIDIZER, NIRP, CLEARLY OUTLINES THE OPERATIONS TO BE FOLLOWED: "THE FIRST STEP IS SELECTION. YOU HAVE TO CHOOSE THE RIGHT PARENT STOCK, MEANING THE ROSE THAT WILL PLAY THE FEMALE WHICH, WHEN FERTILIZED, MATURES THE FRUIT FROM WHICH THE SEEDS ARE TAKEN AND WHICH WILL PLAY THE MALE COUNTERPART AND SUPPLY THE POLLEN. THEN AFTER HAVING GATHERED AND STORED THE "FATHER" POLLEN, YOU MOVE ON TO PREPAR-

ING THE "MOTHER" ROSE. MANUAL POLLINATION CONSISTS OF TRANSFERRING THE FATHER ROSE'S POLLEN ONTO THE MOTHER'S STIGMA AND IS DONE FROM MAY TO JUNE. IF ALL PROCEEDS AS PLANNED, IN AUTUMN THE PLANTS WILL BE FERTILIZED AND WILL PRODUCE THE FALSE FRUITS THAT CONTAIN THE SEEDS. WHEN MADE TO GERMINATE, THESE WILL GIVE LIFE TO A NEW POPULATION OF ROSES THE NEXT YEAR. THESE ROSES WILL BE STRICTLY SELECTED IN THE SUCCEEDING YEARS SO AS TO IDENTIFY THE MOST INTERESTING PLANTS BEST RESEMBLING THE RESULT DESIRED."

THE FIRST HYBRID TEA WAS CREATED IN 1867, ON THE OCCASION OF THE COMPETITION LAUNCHED BY THE HORTICULTURE SOCIETY OF LYON, TO CHOOSE THE FRENCH ROSE THAT WOULD HAVE THE HONOR TO BEAR THE NAME "LA FRANCE." AMONG THE OVER 1,000 VARIETIES EXAMINED, THE PANEL OF JUDGES CHOSE THE ROSE PRESENTED BY JEAN-BAPTISTE GUILLOT. THE HYBRIDIZER FROM LYON, WHO WAS NOT EVEN ABLE TO TRACE ITS LINEAGE — AT THAT TIME, TARGET BREEDING WAS NOT IN VOGUE AND THE MERIT OF THE RESULT WENT ABOVE ALL TO THE POLLINATING INSECTS — "HAD PRODUCED A ROSE WITH STRONG AND UPRIGHT BRANCHES, A RE-FLOWERING ROSE OF A PASTEL PINK COLOR CHARACTERIZED BY AN ABSOLUTELY NEW SHAPE, POINTED BUD AND COROLLA WITH FOLD-BACK PETALS," AS MAURIZIO USAI HIMSELF REPORTED. A DECADE LATER, THANKS ABOVE ALL TO THE WORK OF THE ENGLISHMAN, HENRY BENNET, CROSS-BREEDING ASSUMED AN "ALMOST SCIENTIFIC" TRAIT: THEY STARTED SELECTING THE STOCK OF PARENTS VERY CAREFULLY, AND CROSSBRED THEM WITH THE AIM OF OBTAINING A PROGENY WHICH POSSESSED THE SPECIFIC FEATURES OF ONE AND THE OTHER. IN 1900 THE FRENCH ROSE GROWER, PERNET-DUCHER, OBTAINED IN THIS WAY THE FIRST HYBRID TEA WITH A YELLOW FLOWER, THE "SOLEIL D'OR" CULTIVATED AFTER CROSSBREEDING A HYBRID PERPETUAL AND A PERSIAN *FOETID ROSE*. FROM THEN ON, THE HYBRID TEAS DREW REPEATED SUCCESS, LIKE THAT ACHIEVED AT THE END OF WWII BY A ROSE CROSSBRED BY FRANCIS MEILLAND IN 1942. IT WAS YELLOW SUFFUSED WITH PINK, KNOWN IN GERMANY AS "GLORIA DEI," (LAT. FOR *GLORY OF GOD*) IN FRANCE AS "MADAME A. MEILLAND," AND IN ITALY AS "GIOIA."(IT. FOR *JOY*) IT WAS AWARDED BY THE AMERICAN ROSE SOCIETY ON AUGUST 15, 1945, THE SAME DAY JAPAN SURRENDERED. DUE TO THIS, IN AMERICA IT WAS RENAMED "PEACE," THE ROSE OF PEACE. TODAY THE NUMBER OF SPECIALIZED HYBRIDIZERS OF FLORIST ROSES HAS DECISIVELY INCREASED. BESIDES THE HISTORICAL SIGNATURES OF THE FRENCH MEILLAND, AND

THE GERMAN W. KORDES' SÖHNE AND ROSEN TANTAU, THOSE OF THE DUTCH DE RUITER INNOVATIONS, SCHREURS, LEX+ THE ROSE FACTORY, INTERPLANT ROSES, PREESMAN PLANTS, TERRA NIGRA AND OLIJ ROZEN, AS WELL AS THE FRENCH NIRP AND ENGLISH DAVID AUSTIN, ALSO BECOMING FAMOUS.

AGAIN THE WORDS OF MAURIZIO USAI HAVE COME TO OUR AID IN DETAILING THE NEW TRENDS: "BESIDES BROADENING THE RANGE OF COLORS AND SHADES, THE EFFORT HAS INCREASINGLY FOCUSED ON RECOVERING IN FLORIST ROSES, SOME OF THE TYPICAL, OLD CHARACTERISTICS, SUCH AS THE FLAT, FIVE-PETAL ROSE."

THE HYBRIDS TEAS HAVE FANTASTIC NAMES LIKE AVALANCHE, RED NAOMI!, AND BOHÈME, WHICH IN THE HYBRIDIZERS' CATALOGS ARE PRECEDED BY ALPHANUMERICAL CODES. "THIS NOMENCLATURE IS NECESSARY," EXPLAINS CHARLES LANSDORP, DIRECTOR OF THE DUTCH OFFICE OF FLOWERS IN ITALY, "LIKEWISE, IT IS NECESSARY TO HAVE THE REGISTRATION TRADEMARK WHICH USUALLY FOLLOWS THE TRADE NAME WITH WHICH THE ROSE WILL BE MARKETED. ALL THE NEW VARIETIES OF ROSES AND THEREFORE, ALSO OF HYBRID TEAS, ARE PROTECTED BY A PATENT, FOR A SIMPLE REASON." THE REGISTRATION ALLOWS THE HYBRIDIZERS TO EXERCISE THEIR PROPERTY RIGHTS AND THUS COLLECT ROYALTIES FOR THE EXPLOITATION OF THE PRODUCT FOR COMMERCIAL PURPOSES. SUSCEPTIBLE TO THE WHIMS OF THE MARKET WHICH FOR YEARS HAS BEEN INVADED BY AN EXTENSIVE NUMBER OF NEW VARIETIES, FLORIST ROSES REMAIN, AT LEAST AT EUROPEAN LEVELS, FAITHFUL TO TWO COLORS, WHITE AND RED. OF COURSE THE PALETTE HAS BROADENED AND TODAY, ROSES EXHIBITING MAUVE OR PURPLE COROLLAS ARE GREATLY APPRECIATED, AS ARE THOSE WITH SHADES OF TERRACOTTA AND CHAMOIS.

HOW ABOUT THE STEM LENGTH? ALSO HERE, THE TRENDS SET THE STANDARD. IN ITALY, FOR EXAMPLE, EVEN LONG-STEMMED ROSES OVER 39.3 IN (100 CM), WHICH WERE VERY POPULAR 10 YEARS AGO, HAVE GIVEN WAY TO SHORTER STEMS.

THERE IS ALSO THE CURIOUS ISSUE OF PERFUME. PERFUMED FLORIST ROSES ARE RARE, SINCE THE FRAGRANCE MAKES THEM MORE DELICATE AND MORE PERISHABLE. HOWEVER, RESEARCH BY SOME HYBRIDIZERS HAVE BEEN ENCOURAGING LATELY... AND SOON PERHAPS, THE SWEET PERFUME OF ROSE PETALS THAT PERVADES OUR GARDENS, WILL NO LONGER BE THE PREROGATIVE OF ONLY A FEW VARIETIES.

1 Red Paris, hybridized by the Dutch company, Olij Rozen.   2-3 Isis, hybridized by the Dutch company, Schreurs.   4-5 Green Beauty, hybridized by the Dutch company, Olij Rozen.
6-7 Cherry Brandy, hybridized by the German company, Rosen Tantau.

*"Bouquet of the Soul"*

"We possess our soul once in a while./Nobody has it continually /and forever ..." so goes a famous verse of the poem "Talking about the soul" composed by the Polish poet Wisława Szymborska (1923-2012), Nobel Prize for Literature in 1996. Fleeting, ethereal, white, the soul inevitably recalls another imperManent image : that of white roses. Symbol of grace and beauty, the roses in the variety of this color truly have a very special meaning.

Say white and you immediately call to mind snow, ice, the dawn, the clouds, milk, a sheet, awaiting to receive a story to be told. Due to an inexplicable "domino of words" white becomes, in people's imagination, light, infinity, the soul, perfection, but also innocence, bounty, purity and eternal love.

At times it is dazzling, at times powdery, then almost transparent; white is one of the favorite colors of rose lovers. Defined by the theory of colors as a "non color," since it sums up all the seven that compose the solar spectrum, it offers, generally in flowers, and in the Tea hybrids, an almost infinite range of shades. An example of this is the bouquet dedicated to the roses "of the soul" which anticipate the varieties presented in this section and mixes pure white to powder-cream, transiting through a very pale lemon green. Margherita Angelucci of *Foglie, fiori e fantasia* of Milan, who created the bouquet explained : "I wanted to demonstrate that even in the florists' roses, as in nature, there is no white, but a rainbow of whites".

White roses are protagonists in weddings, where they are the symbol of pure love and fidelity and are ideal in creating romantic bridal bouquets. They also act as *boutonnière* or buttonhole flowers of the spouse and the best man. They become the perfect gift for a birth, a baptism, communion or christening, or on any special occasion. On the other hand, white evokes innocence, life that is beginning or is transformed.

Magical, full of poetry and suggestion, white roses exhibit swirling buds that open to give us cup-shaped flowers or rosettes with big corollas, even 4.7 in (12 cm) in diameter. Their petals are of a gentle texture resembling satin, organdy and velvet; long straight stems up to 35.4 in (90 cm) long and beautiful dark green leaves that often create a particular depth against the overtones of the corolla. Rarely fragrant, they give their best in the unbelievable palette of colors they can offer. Fruit of long and constant research work, at times involving hybridizers for years, they fan out a range of tones that go from the pure white of roses like the Akito, Dolomiti, Tibet and White Lydia, to white with a touch of green as in Avalanche + and White Naomi !, to the cream of Mondial and Vendela. To reach, passing through a variety of the clearest lemon green of Emerald Avalanche, Green Beauty, Green Tea and Jade, to the white-cream-apricot of Crème de la crème, to the beige-pink of La Belle, up to champagne-powder of Talea+. And when the white-cream mixes with the red rose, the result is stunning, as we can see in Bohème, Cézanne, Friendship and Sweetness.

12-13 Forty roses of four different varieties for this magical bouquet which blends the white of Avalanche+ and White Lydia roses to the pale lemon-green of the Emerald Avalanche and the creamy almost powdery shades of Talea+. To give an impression of motion to this composition, olive branches were used of a delicate shade halfway between green sage and grey silver, reflecting the nuances of the bouquet's colors.    14 The Mondial rose hybridized by the German company, W. Kordes' Söhne.

# *Jade*

This rose is called "Jade," one of the most precious ornamental stones. Found among the artifacts of the Ne-olithic Age, the ancient Chinese considered it a sacred stone, full of virtues. It is used in Crystal therapy for its soothing, balancing and harmonizing properties. In Chinese culture it is still the most romantic gift a lover can ever give his beloved. Furthermore, its green heart with white veins or pink-streaks, in ayurvedic tradition is as-sociated to the fourth chakra, that of the heart. And this rose, created by Rosen Tantau (Germany) also recalls love, and the emotion of the most romantic declarations. Poetic and charming, it is cultivated in Africa and South America. Its medium-sized flower opens out with a diameter of 2.7-3.1 in (7-8 cm) and blooms on a stem of 15.7-27.5 in (40-70 cm).

PRECIOUS AS A GEM

PERFECT
FOR A WHITE DAY

# *Akito*

In Japan, White Day is celebrated on March 14, exactly a month after St. Valentine's Day. The celebration "obliges" lovers, engaged men and husbands to give a sweet and white gift to their beloved, as a thank you token for the gift received on February 14. This uniquely Japanese habit has specific rules. The male reciprocates with a small gift, mostly marshmallows and strictly white chocolates, if the gift received was inexpensive. For expensive gifts, the options are flowers, clothes or jewelry. Also in Japan, especially among the ladies of the imperial family, these roses, bred by Rosen Tantau (Germany) with their pure, almost optic white petals, are a perfect gift for White Day. Cultivated in South America, it has an open corolla of 2.7-3.1 in (7-8 cm) and a stem 19.6-27.5 in (50-70 cm) long. They are cultivated in Italy, France and Netherlands.

# Cézanne

A painter of poetry, the French artist Paul Cézanne rarely painted flowers. His favorite subjects were landscapes, still nature and whole figure portraits. And yet this rose was named after the artist, in memory of some of his color matches, like white and red, able to express not only the emotion of the observer but also the essence of the subject painted. It is precisely the tones of Cézanne's still nature paintings that seem to have inspired the hybrid rose of Olij Rozen (Netherlands). Its white-cream petals in fact have an elegant, curled edge with cyclamen-pink overtones almost bordering with red, ever more intense and determined. A big flower, it opens out to measure 3.9-4.7 in (10-12 cm). Cézanne has a long stem of 19.6-31.5 in (50-80 cm) and the most beautiful heart-shaped dark-green leaves. It is cultivated in Netherlands and South America.

WHEN COLOR
TURNS INTO POETRY

# *Crème de la Crème*

On July 2, 2011, the wedding of Albert of Monaco and Charlène Wittstock was celebrated in the courtyard of the Royal Palace of Monaco. The princely ceremony counted over 3,500 guests consisting of celebrities, politicians and royalty, further honored by very elegant floral decor, in which roses were the protagonists. Over 9,000 of three different varieties : Crème de la crème, hybridized by Rosen Tantau (Germany) ; Mondial, hybridized by W. Kordes' Söhne (Germany) and Anastasia, hybridized by Nirp International (France). Three roses are cataloged "white," but each of a different type of white. Crème de la crème, in fact has a warm, almost peach colored heart, whereas Anastasia is dazzling snow white and Mondial tones down to shades of powdery cream-green. Crème de la crème is a big flowered rose with an opening of 3.9-4.7 in (10-12 cm) and a stem with length of 19.6-31.5 in (50-80 cm).

IN THE ROYAL
PRINCIPATE
OF MONACO

# Dolomiti

The Dolomites were formed 200 million years ago and today soar up to the sky at an altitude of over 3,000 m. They are considered one of the most beautiful mountains in the world and in 2009 were declared a World Heritage Site by UNESCO. This elegant and sophisticated rose is dedicated to these rock cathedrals, set against the pureness of snow which enshrouds them in winter as in a fable. Created by Olij Rozen (Netherlands), its petals are very close to icy, almost optical white, and the outer ones just slightly streaked with green, conceal a heart of warm, cream-powder tones. A great effect is the chromatic contrast amid the shades of the corolla, and the dark green and shiny leaves. Formed by 40 petals with an opening of 3.9-4.7 in (10-12 cm), Dolomiti has a stem of 19.6-35.4 in (50-90 cm). It is cultivated in Netherlands, France and Italy.

DREAMING OF THE HIGHLANDS

# Green Beauty

The cut and color of its petals, created by a Korean hybridizer and today marketed by Olij Rozen (Netherlands), suggests the image of spring. A transitional season in nature as in life, spring is the time for beauty, rebirth and transformation, and as the trees are filled with shoots waiting to dress up its foliage in green, also as the youth take their first steps into the world, waiting to become adults. Fresh, pert, a bit frou-frou, Green Beauty exhibits a corolla of delicate green hues, toning down to light, dusty pink. Ideal for all types of bouquets, and a perfect homage to a young, modern and dynamic woman, Green Beauty has a flower of 35-40 petals and on opening measures 2.7-3.1 in (7-8 cm) in diameter, with a stem of 15.7-31.5 in (40-80 cm).

FROM KOREA WITH LOVE

# *Bohème*

ON THE NOTES
OF PUCCINI

Dedicated to the famous opera of Giacomo Puccini, this rose was inspired by the romantic retro atmosphere of Paris in the 1830s, with its Bohemian artists and Mimi, the flower embroiderer, in love with Rodolfo, one of the youthful protagonists of the novel in Henri Murger's *Scénes de la vie de bohème* on which Puccini, Giuseppe Giacosa and Luigi Illica based the libretto. Delicate and with an almost devastating beauty, this rose has 35 petals, a cream color with an intense pink border, a big swirling bud, a stem that can reach 35.4 in (90 cm) and very few thorns. It has a slight but persistent perfume. Its corolla when open, measures 3.9 in (10 cm) in diameter. Bred by NIRP International (France), it is cultivated mostly in Italy and Kenya.

# *Tibet*

The thin air, the Himalayan chain and its highest mountain, the Everest, monks, prayers entrusted to the wind and the teachings of Buddha, on one hand, lead to the ambition of reaching the peak, and on the other, to getting closer to God, the soul and the essence before life. This rose which bears the name of one of the most beautiful and inaccessible Asian regions, with the pureness of its petals and the perfect shape of its corolla, forcefully expresses the image of purity, spirituality and of man who aspires perfection. Hybridized by Olij Rozen (Netherlands), Tibet is an incredible snow white rose, which opens out to 3.9-4.7 in (10-12 cm) and has a long stem of 19.6-31.5 in (50-80 cm). Grown in South America, it is one of the most used roses in weddings, births and communions.

# White Lydia

If you look at a White Lydia bouquet from above, it appears almost as if a shower of pure snowflakes was scattered over a green cushion. Fruit of careful and accurate research in crossbreeding, this roses resembles in all ways its cousins growing in the garden. The experts call them Spray. These are branched roses meaning that each branch divides into at least two or three thinner stems, which in turn branch into other, even thinner stems. The result? A branch of White Lydia can count up to more than 10 flowers. Created by Interplant Roses, the Dutch hybridizer specializing in Spray roses, it gives milky-white flowers with a stem of 15.7-23.6 in (40-60 cm) and is very much used in flower décor for weddings, in place of the Gypsophila.

FASCINATING LIKE
A GARDEN ROSE

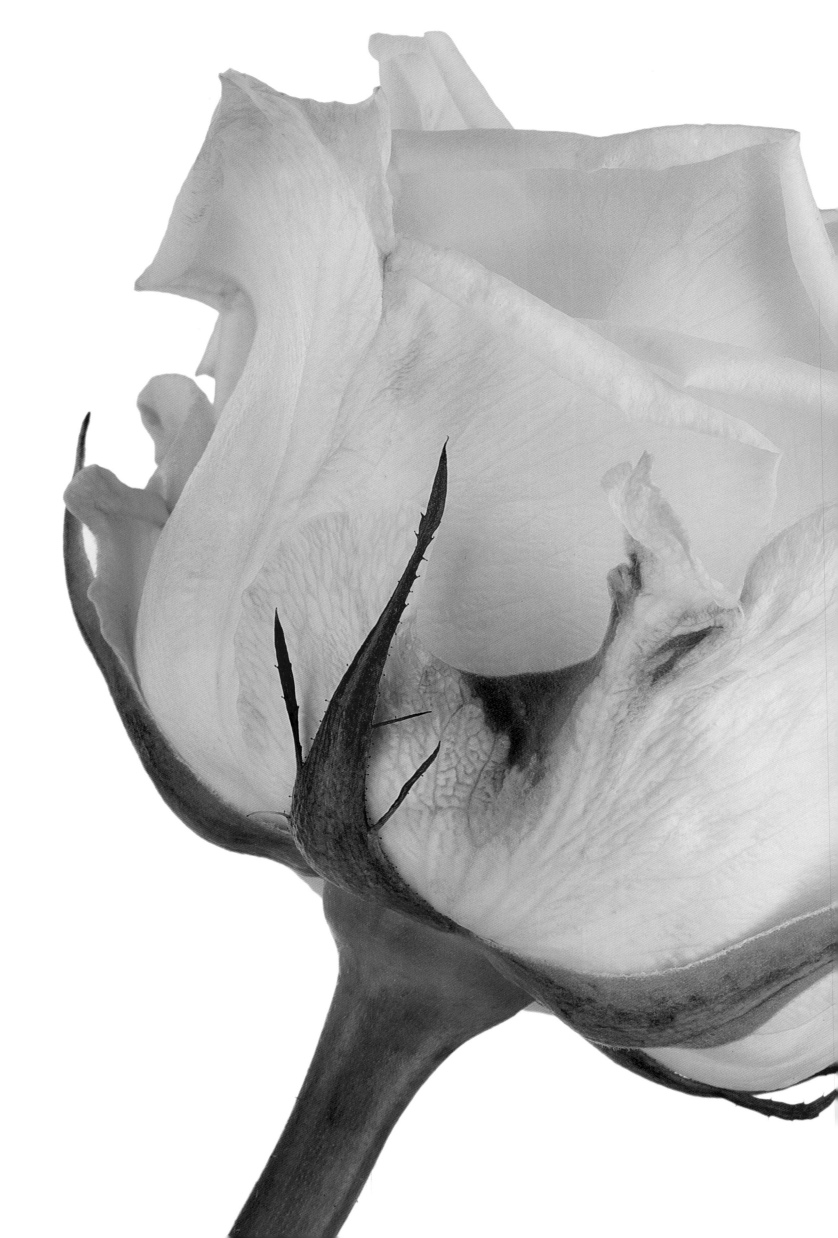

# *White Naomi!*

For his 40th birthday, the then engaged Russian millionaire, Vladislav Doronin, gave her a gigantic bunch of White Naomis! The white rose bearing her name has become over a few years, the favorite of *flower designers* worldwide. We are obviously referring to Naomi Campbell, the English top model defined by *People* magazine as one of the 50 most beautiful women in the world and the inspiration of Schreurs, Dutch hybridizer who dedicated to her also this variety, among the other famous ones, Naomi! and Red Naomi! Refined, charming and delicately perfuse, this rose's color, ranging from white and cream toned down to green, has a corolla opening of 3.5-4.3 in (9-11 cm), a stem 23.6-35.4 in (60-90 cm) long and a fantastic green foliage that creates an effective chromatic contrast with the overtones of the petals.

# WHOEVER DRESSES IN GREEN...

... places her trust in her beauty, says a famous proverb. And yet, there is no season in which fashion shows do not exhibit dresses and accessories of this wonderful color, expressed according to the whims of stylists, in the most varied shades of emerald, turquoise, aquamarine, musk and sage. This "green mania," for some years now, has contaminated even the hybridizers who have created gorgeous roses with green blooms, as if to defy the proverb. Emerald Avalanche for example, created by the Dutch, Lex+ the Rose Factory, is a recent mutation of the famous Avalanche+ cultivar. It took its size and bearing from its sister, but displays a delicate lemon-green corolla, a very spring-fresh color, most fitting to this big rose which is more than 4.7 in (12 cm) when open, with a stem of 25.5-35.4 in (65-90 cm).

*Emerald
Avalanche*

# Talea+

In 2004, Talea+ won the Fleur Primeur, a recognition that could be considered a sort of floral Grammy Award, promoted yearly by Flora Holland to award the most beautiful flowers of the world. What made it so special, so as to win the title, was mainly its really unique color, a champagne-cream toned down into a warm and delicate shade of powder-pink, and thus, international fame was earned. Its particular nuance in fact, lights up when matched with whites, making its pink even more romantic and extremely warm when combined with orange gradations and autumn leaves. Most loved by *flower designers* who choose it as the protagonist of bridal bouquets or compositions for baptisms, communions, christenings and special occasions, this rose created by Lex+ the Rose Factory (Netherlands) has a big flower of 4.7 in (12 cm) in diameter and opens out like a crown on a stem that is 23.6-31.5 in (60-80 cm) long.

TEMPERAMENTAL LIKE A STAR

# Friendship

A human necessity for Aristotle, and comfort for Antoine de Saint-Exupéry (author of *The Little Prince* who wrote : "My friend, by your side I have nothing to ask pardon for, or defend myself with, nothing to demonstrate : I find peace... beyond my poor words you can see just a man in me."), friendship is a deep experience and of an inestimable value for individuals and society as a whole. Created by Meilland International (France) for the tenth anniversary of the tragic events of September 11, 2001, this rose was called Friendship to convey a message of peace and brotherhood amongst peoples. In its petals in fact, the inner red matches with streaks of crimson on the outside, creating a total, grandiose harmony. A big flower, it opens out to 3.9-4.7 in (10-12 cm), and has a long stem of 23.6-31.5 in (60-80 cm). It is cultivated in France.

# La Belle

Once upon a time, a handsome and selfish prince was transformed by an enchantment, into a monstrous beast. This is the opening line of the film *The Beauty and the Beast,* a cartoon produced by Disney Pictures in 1991. The duration of the enchantment – in order not be trapped in the role of the Beast, the prince will fall in love, on his 21st birthday – is marked by a rose that will bloom up to that day, after which it will wither and eternally condemn him to a monstrous existence. Romantic, delicate, with its petals shaded down to green and pink, this variety cross-bred by W. Kordes' Söhne (Germany) does not makes us think of the red rose of the enchantment but because of its bounty, beauty and virtues of Belle, recall the young protagonist of the Disney fable who will save the prince. A big flower, it opens out to measure 3.9-4.7 in (10-12 cm), with a stem of 23.6-35.4 in (60-90 cm).

# *Green Tea* A WHIFF OF THE ORIENT

For several years now, green tea of Chinese origin and prepared with the undried leaves of *Camelia sinensis,* has crossed the confines of the Asian continent and conquered the West. This success is firstly due to its tonic virtues which, though not exciting, stimulate intellectual functions, helps digestion and has a high vitamin C content. It furthermore possesses recognized and appreciated qualities : taste, perfume, and last but not least, color. A delicate and unique lemon green, it brings to mind the first gems of spring, which in the corolla of this rose created by Rosen Tantau (Germany), becomes even more vibrant in the texture of its petals. A big flower, swirling bud, with a stem of 23.6-35.4 in (60-90 cm), Green Tea has few thorns, a light but persistent fragrance and fantastic green leaves. It is cultivated in Netherlands, France and Italy.

# *Vendela*

## THE ELEGANT ONE WHO SOMETIMES DRESSES IN BLUE

The Vendela is known as the rose for weddings, but most ignore the fact that the much loved or detested (according to taste) blue roses belong to this genre. In fact, just immerse the stem in a colored water solution to tinge its corolla perfectly, making it electric blue or night cobalt. The Dutch, always so inventive, even manage to give a different color to each of its petals. Crossbred in Netherlands in the 1990s, by Rosen Tantau (Germany),this rose was and still is very popular today the world over, especially in the Italian market. The merit mainly goes to its characteristics : a big flower, delicate, dusty-cream color, pretty green leaves, and a stem of 35.4 in (90 cm). It is cultivated in Italy, Netherlands and Colombia.

# *Avalanche+*

The name could not fit better : this rose in fact, not only endows us with 400 flowering stems per sq m of culti-vation, but has an extraordinarily long blooming period. Crossbred by Lex Voorn (Netherlands), today it is one of the most popular roses used for bridal bouquets and floral decorations for weddings. It has accompanied Dutch princesses to the altar – such as Maxima of Netherlands – and actresses and models – like Yolanthe Cabau van Kasbergen who married the Dutch soccer player Wesley Sneijder in 2010. With big flowers of pure, almost snowy white with a touch of green, this rose is more than 4.7 in (12 cm) in diameter when open, and its stem is 25.5-35.4 in (65-90 cm) long, with beautiful green leaves. Surprisingly, Avalanche+ is long-enduring in the vase, even in summer.

# *Sweetness*

White with pink edges, at first glance it recalls the cheeks of a young girl, soft and light to touch like a silk scarf, and the notes of a melodic love song. Created by Rosen Tantau (Germany), Sweetness is a mutation of the famous Noblesse cultivar, the rose in vogue in Italy at the turn of the 1980s. Cultivated in Ecuador, Mexico and Colombia, it tops the list of the ten most loved roses in Eastern Europe, headed by Russia. A lucky feature is its long stem of 35.4 in (90 cm) and its big flower which opens to measure over 4.7 in (12 cm). Standards of beauty are today considered most essential by Russian consumers, but it is no longer so for the Italians who choose roses with long stems almost only to celebrate special anniversaries like St. Valentine's Day.

WHEN SUCCESS IS WRITTEN IN ITS DNA

# *Mondial*

This was the rose Charlène Wittstock and Albert of Monaco chose for the floral decorations of their nuptial rites celebrated in Monte Carlo on July 2, 2011. Hybridized by W. Kordes' Söhne (Germany) this rose is one of the most preferred by brides all over the world. It is romantic and with a magnificent cup-shaped flower, designed by a vortex of soft and sensual petals of an original color, with cream shades that blend with a touch of pale pink and water green. Cultivated mostly in South Africa, it is the favorite of *flower designers*, who today use it to create magical bouquets of all types, sealed only by a satin ribbon or by a pearl. It is characterized by a big flower (its opening measures 3.9-4.7 in (10-12 cm), stem of 27.5 in (70 cm), leaves of intense green without thorns and an emission of delicate fragrance.

*"Bouquet of the Sun"*

Life is tough for yellow roses. In flower language, yellow has always symbolized jealousy, betrayal and uncertain love. In addition as hybridizers say, yellow roses are a real feat to achieve. Yellow is considered sacred by Buddhists who associate it to wisdom. It is one of the preferred colors of impressionist artists like Henri Matisse and Paul Gauguin, and some representatives of abstract art like Joan Miró who in his works, for example, chose the most saturated tones, that of pure yellow, immune from any sort of chromatic contamination. But yellow is also the color of the sun, gold, light and joy. And precisely the significance of yellow was what inspired the bouquets created by Margherita Angelucci for the section dedicated to these roses. The Milanese florist said, "I imagined the light of the sun, and thought of showing this in the various moments of the day." So next to the Ilios with their gentle yellow-green that evokes dawn and the grazing light of the morning in a crescendo of chromatic intensities, we find the Sphinx roses with their intense sand-yellow that calls to mind the warmest moments of the day when the ball of fire is at its zenith and its rays are burning, and then the Milva flowers of a very original orange-red, and the Coffee Breaks with their very attractive terracotta rust, reminding us of the beauty and intensity of light at sunset, when the rays set the sky afire.

In reality, the yellow roses we know are inspired by the complete range of minerals found in nature : cadmium, chrome, zinc, Indian yellow and Saturn red. The hues are difficult to achieve as we said, for two reasons : firstly because the intense color of the bud fades away once the rose opens and, furthermore, because some of the less desired traits of the parent stocks tend to resurface. The first yellow Hybrid Tea rose in history was that of the "Soleil d'Or" cultivar. Fruit of the work of French hybridizer, Pernet-Ducher, this rose, achieved in 1900, was the legitimate offspring of a perpetual hybrid, "Antoine Ducher" and a Persian foetid rose. From then on, since a bit of the blood of "Soleil d'Or" flows in the veins of all yellow roses, it may sometimes occur that the leaves are pale green like those of the Persian foetid rose : considered a defect by hybridizers who moreover, consider the work laborious and often resulting in unsuccessful propagation of these roses.

So this is why the roses presented in this section are so precious. They successfully overcame the hazards of multiplication in identical numbers, and despite the meanings they are attributed with, convey such overwhelming sunny sensations. Intense, vibrant and exuberant, yellow roses are the perfect homage to the most extrovert of people. As always, the range of gradations and tones of the color palettes covered by these roses are really incredibly surprising encompassing the lightest yellow, just slightly tinged with the pink of the Aubade, the pale but luminous yellow of Limbo, the pastel hue of the Butterscotch, Senegal yellow just lightly streaked with the green of Leonidas, the peach of Finesse, sand-ocher of Mohana, dark ocher of Leonidas up to the rusty-yellow of Mariyo !, the red-orange of Cherry Brandy and Milva and, to conclude, the extraordinary terracotta of Coffee Break.

74-75  In these bouquets by *Foglie, fiori e fantasia*, the Ilios and Sphinx yellow blends with the orange red of Milva and the terracotta of the Coffee Break roses, with the shades of the latter repeated in the green utilized in the magnolia leaves at the bottom of the page.   76  The Limbo rose, hybridized by the German company, W. Kordes' Söhne.

# Butterscotch

In flower language, the yellow rose is the symbol of jealousy. If the yellow is fiery and intense, it stands for doubt and if the shades are lighter, for uncertainty in love. Yet, yellow is the color of the sun and is by definition a positive valence. On the other hand, even modern color therapy which studied the effects of the vibrations emanated by colors on the psycho-physical states of people, confirms that yellow gives energy, strength and vitality. It brings joy and when it has a delicate, pastel shade, like that of this rose created by Olij Rozen (Netherlands), it effuses sweetness, exactly as occurs with Butterscotch candy, a famous sugar and butter *bon bon*, which gave this rose its name. A medium-sized rose, when open it has a diameter of 2.7-3.1 in (7-8 cm) and a stem 19.6-35.4 in (50-90 cm) long.

UTTERLY SWEET
LIKE CANDY

# *Aubade*

*Aubade*, the morning serenade, is a theme much loved by the French tradition. It was also re-proposed by Pablo Picasso in 1967 in a painting which was given this title. The morning serenade is a magical moment for lovers, languid and also full of nostalgia : man, after a night of love, greets his beloved dedicating to her a beautiful and romantic song. Slightly fragrant and with few thorns, this rose cultivar with petals ranging from yellow cream with pink borders, recalls the dawn and the first rays of the sun, and takes inspiration from this magical instant. Elegant and full of charm, Aubade counts 40 petals and when open, its diameter is about 4.7 in (12 cm) with a stem that can reach up to 23.6-27.5 in (60-70 cm) in length. Hybridized by NIRP International (France), it has become a success over the last few years and is cultivated especially in Ecuador and exported worldwide.

MORNING SERENADE

# *Sphinx*

Present in both Egyptian and Greek mythology and depicted with the body of a lion and the face of a man, the sphinx has by now become the collective idea of the symbol of mystery and enigmas. Precisely the Sphinx (the sacred monument located close to the Giza pyramids in Egypt is famous) inspired this rose, created by Dutch company, Preesman Plants. Of a warm yellow-gold color that evokes the blinding light of the sun at its zenith, ancient Egypt and the spectacular settings of Zeffirelli's *Aida*, this flower opens out to 2.7-3.1 in (7-8 cm) and has a stem 15.7-27.5 in (40-70 cm) in length, completely thornless. Really impressive is the chromatic contrast between the shades of the corolla against the dark green of the leaves. It is cultivated in Netherlands and South America.

AMID MYTHOLOGY AND MYSTERY

# Cherry Brandy

The British tone of this rose immediately brings us to the English countryside, fox hunts, cottages with the fireplace alight, wood and leather furniture, the smell of tobacco and rites of brandy. In effect, both the name and color of this splendid Hybrid Tea created by Rosen Tantau (Germany) is inspired by the warm hue of the famous liqueur prepared with cherries. Its intense red-orange along the edges of the petals and gradation to lighter shades, almost sun-yellow at the inner part, give it a special glow. A big flower which when open can exceed 4.7 in (12 cm) in diameter, Cherry Brandy has a stem of 19.6-27.5 in (50-70 cm) and beautiful, dark-green, heart-shaped leaves that enhance the particular shades of its corolla.

PETALS THAT TASTE OF CHERRY

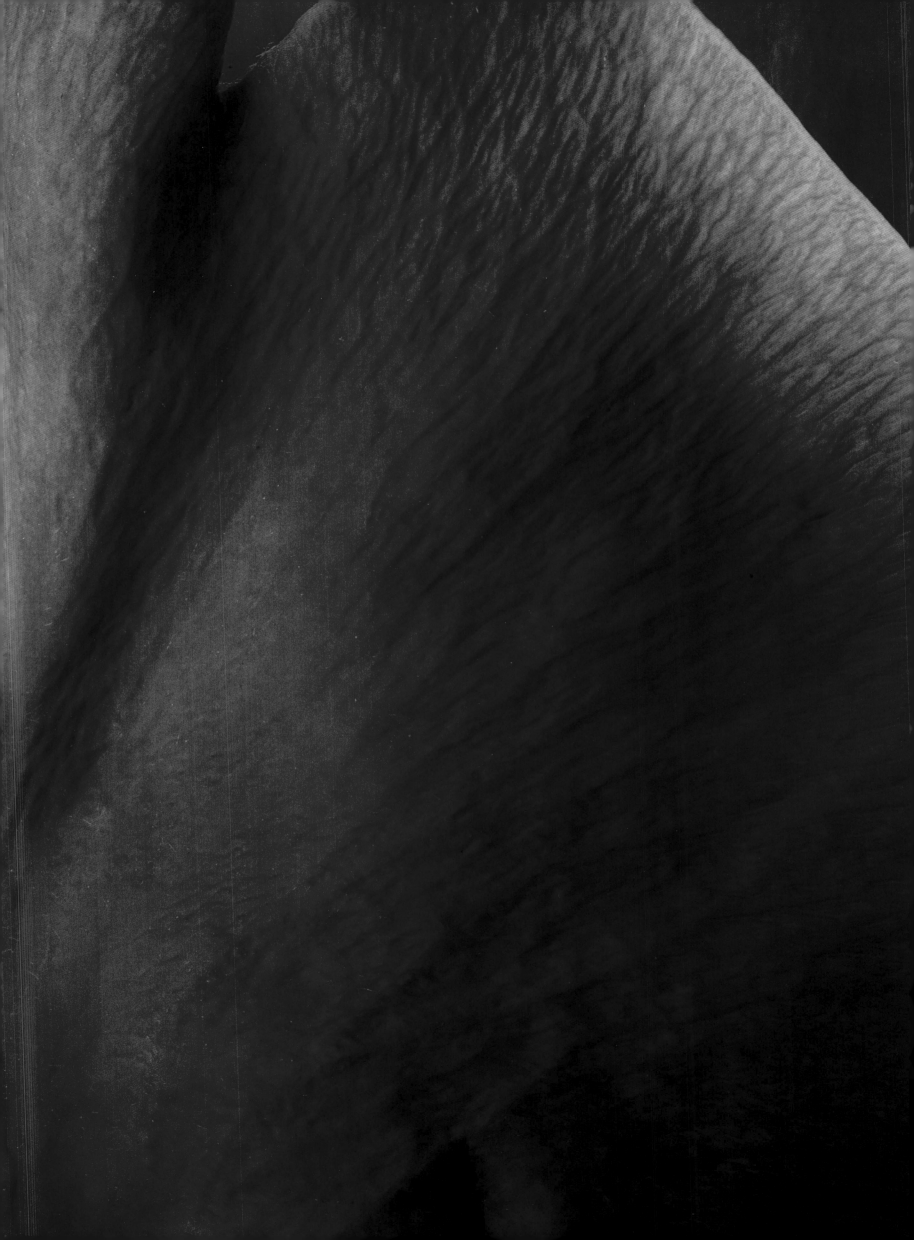

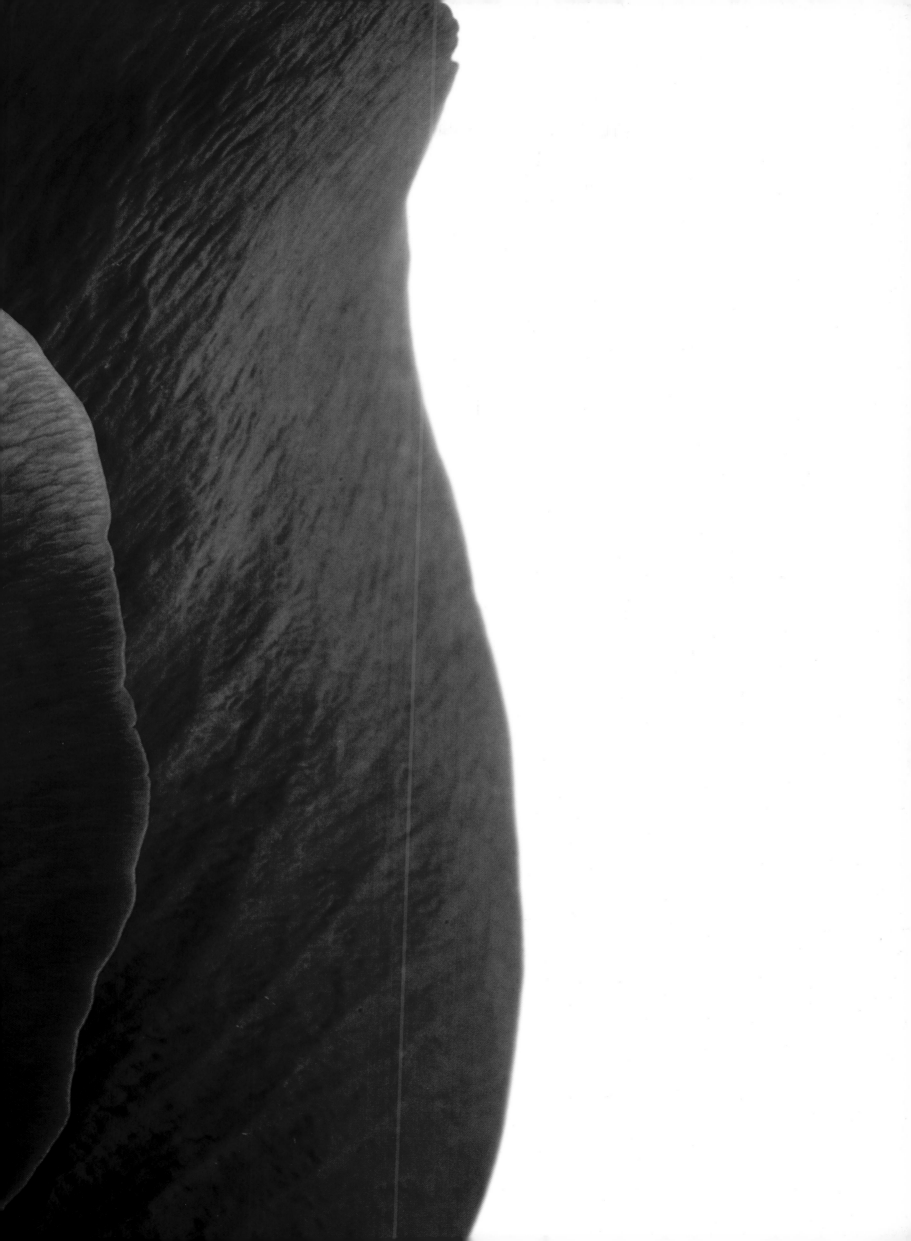

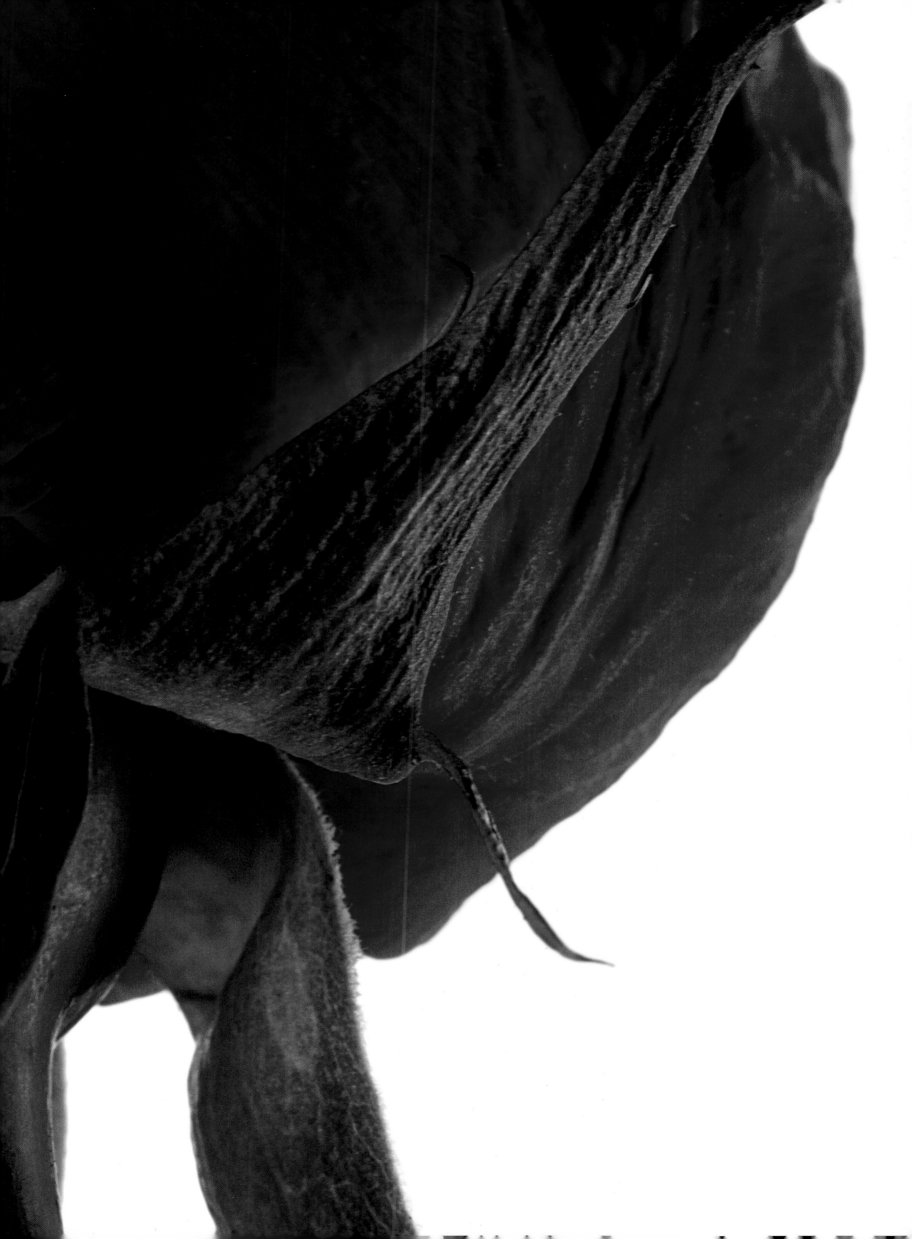

A TRIBUTE TO THE
PANTHER OF GORO

# *Milva La Rossa*

Maria Ilva Biolcati, in art known as Milva or the "Panther of Goro," is one of the most important Italian theater singers and interpreters. Famous the world over, she has been and still is popular in Germany, where she not only won two golden disks, but was awarded the Order of Merit of the Federal Republic of Germany. An outstanding interpreter of Brecht's pieces, she has performed in many German cities, reaping great success and acclaim from the public and critics. Not surprisingly therefore, the cultivator, Rosen Tantau (Germany), thought of paying her a tribute with this rose of a carrot-red color which recalls that of the singer's hair. A big flower, Milva when open surpasses 4.7 in (12 cm) in diameter, and has a stem that measures 19.6-31.5 in (50-80 cm). It is cultivated in France, Italy, Netherlands and South America.

# *Finess*

## TRIUMPH OF PEACH

If we were to associate roses with various types of women, we would say that the white ones, so elegant and refined, have an incomparable aura. The reds have the presumption of being the most beautiful and the yellows denote awareness of the difficulty of being loved, and due to this are the symbols of jealousy. But the peach roses stand apart : their fascination is something special. Gentle, full of grace, they make you think of beauty that has just blossomed, gay and carefree, like this rose characterized by a flower that almost resembles a peony : 40 pink-peach petals on the inside and green on the outside, that open out thickly to create a soft, full and floating, round corolla. Finess has a long stem of 19.6-31.5 in (50-80 cm), and was created by De Ruiter Innovations (Netherlands) and cultivated in Europe and South America.

A MYTH THAT
SETS THE TREND

# Ilios

When Dutch hybridizer, Schreurs, chose the name for this rose, he must have thought it was beautiful, like the sun which daily enlightens our day with its rays, and like Helen, the mythical queen of Troy, the eternal symbol of feminine beauty. It is an overpowering beauty, able to make strong emotions explode, like in the abduction of Helen and the ensuing war, and the desire to possess her, in the case of Ilios in the myth of Homer. This rose in fact, has two features : its color which combines the sage green of its outer petals to warm, Senegal yellow of the inner ones, and the soft shape of its corolla, that seems like a spiral of silk ribbons. Ilios has more than 35 petals and when open measures 3.5-4.3 in (9-11 cm) with a stem of 23.6-35.4 in (60-90 cm).

INSPIRED BY THE DIVINE COMEDY

# *Limbo*

In Dante Alighieri's *Divine Comedy,* Limbo is the first circle of Hell. Here the poet set the castle of the *magnanimous spirits*, the men who had lived justly like Homer, Horace, Ovid and other great pagans. The castle in which the souls live is surrounded by a tiny river and enwrapped in a glow of light. An uncertain, indefinite and suspended place par excellence (the only enlightened circle among Dante's circles), Limbo could not have been better represented than by this rose cross-bred by W. Kordes' Söhne (Germany). Its petals amid the yellow-green not only recalls the light of Dante's castle, but the color gradations are a perfect example of the undefined concept. With a flower opening out to 3.9-4.7 in (10-12 cm), and a stem of 23.6-35.4 in (60-90 cm), Limbo is cultivated in Netherlands.

# *Leonidas*

The French hybridizer, Meilland International, defined the tones of this rose, creating that dark pinkish ocher on the interior and yellow-cream outside, which underline a particularity : when open, the shades of the corolla become more intense and tend towards chocolate. In truth, given that it is called by the same name as a famous brand of Belgian chocolates, the designer label of a delicious praline prepared with first quality ingredients, in the minds of the more greedy chocolate lovers, the association with the so-called "food for the gods" certainly did not go unnoticed. On the other hand, excellence revives excellence, and amid the double faced roses, Leonidas fears no rivals. To its advantage, besides the color, is its cone bud which opens out to a rosette, a long stem of 19.6-27.5 in (50-70 cm), and luxuriant opaque-green foliage. It is cultivated in Italy, France and South America.

DOUBLE-FACE AND SWEET
LIKE CHOCOLATE

# *Mohana*

The Ecuadorian hybridizer who created this rose, has always loved boats, regattas, the high seas and waves of Haiti, his favorite holiday destination, so much so that he repeated every time upon returning : "they are unpredictable, difficult to manage, yet so beautiful, and, I would say, enchanting. This love for the sea inspired the name of this rose which in Maori language means "ocean," a pure fantasy which does not evoke forms, colors, objects or personages but just a tribute to nature and its most beautiful expressions. Today this variety is produced by Rosen Tantau (Germany) and is most loved not only for its warm hues ranging between sand and ocher, but also for its big flower which surpasses 4.7 in (12 cm) in diameter, and a stem 23.6-35.4 in (60-90 cm) long.

ENCHANTING LIKE
AN OCEAN WAVE

# *Mariyo!*

Cadmium yellow and sulfur, orange and coral, rust and sanguine, its petals are the exaltation of the colors of the sun, and call to mind orange trees loaded with fruit in the Sicilian plain of Catania. Created by the Dutch hybridizer, Schreurs, and first-born of another famous cultivar, the Marie-Claire!, this rose has a number of interesting features. It is attractive, counts up to 45 petals, and has a stem that is 31.5 in (80 cm) long. In addition, it is easy to cultivate, is productive (grows almost 300 stems per sq m) and furthermore, is strong (its bud does not perish easily and wears well when transported). Grown mostly in Africa and sent to markets all over the world, it forcedly undergoes hours of flights, and yet arrives at the destination perfect and ready for confectioning in refined bouquets with an autumnal aura.

PERFECT EVEN AFTER JET LAG

# Coffee Break

Coffee breaks are important moments for workers : you take a break, have a chat or two with colleagues while enjoying a hot, invigorating cup of coffee. It takes just a few minutes and you return to work renewed, ready to face all the appointments the day holds in store. With an intense hue that combines ochre gradations to the tones of terracotta and rust, this hybrid rose created by Rosen Tantau (Germany), draws inspiration precisely from *coffee breaks*. Its big corolla opens out to 4.7 in (12 cm) and has a stem of 19.6-27.5 in (50-70 cm). It is most appreciated by *flower designers* especially for its color that recalls the magical show given by the foliage of Canadian maples, and is the protagonist of autumn bouquets.

INVIGORATING LIKE A GOOD CUP OF COFFEE

"Bouquet of the Heart"

RED, PINK AND MAUVE. THESE ARE THE COLORS OF THIS BOUQUET THAT OPENS THE SECTION DEDICATED TO THE ROSES "OF THE HEART." THREE TONES, THREE MEANINGS, BUT ONLY ONE RED THREAD: A SENTIMENT THAT TURNS INTO PASSION, LOVE AND DESIRE FOR KNOWLEDGE.

RED IS MUCH MORE THAN A COLOR; IT IS ALMOST AN IDEA, SO MUCH SO THAT IT IDENTIFIES ITSELF WITH THE OBJECT TO WHICH IT ENDOWS ITS WARM, ENERGETIC AND VIBRANT HUES.

EYE-CATCHING, INTENSE, AND STIMULATING, IT ENCOMPASSES IN ITSELF THE *YIN* AND *YANG*, DAY AND NIGHT, MALE AND FEMALE AND GOOD AND EVIL. RED IS BLOOD WHICH GIVES LIFE AND DEATH. RED IS FIRE THAT WARMS AND BURNS, BUT RED IS ALSO LOVE. IT IS NO SURPRISE, THEREFORE, IF IN THE LANGUAGE OF FLOWERS, THE RED ROSE HAS ALWAYS BEEN THE SYMBOL OF PASSIONATE LOVE. OSCAR WILDE, FOR EXAMPLE, IN *THE NIGHTINGALE AND THE ROSE* WROTE: "... YOU SAID YOU WOULD DANCE WITH ME, THE STUDENT SAID. SO HERE IS THE REDDEST ROSE IN THE WORLD. I WILL PIN IT CLOSE TO YOUR HEART AND WHILE WE DANCE, IT WILL TELL YOU HOW MUCH I LOVE YOU."

RED IS THE MOST LOVED COLOR TOGETHER WITH WHITE, IN FRESH CUT ROSES. FROM CARDINAL RED TO REDDISH PURPLE, GERANIUM TO LACQUER RED AND RUBY TO CRIMSON, IT BECOMES THE FLOWER PAR EXCELLENCE ON ST. VALENTINE'S DAY. IT DOES NOT MATTER IF THE PERSON GIVING IT CHOOSES JUST ONE OR A DOZEN. WHAT COUNTS IS THAT THE VARIETY CHOSEN BEARS THE NAME OF ONE OF THE PRETTIEST: EL TORO, GRAND PRIX, RED NAOMI!, RED PARIS AND PASSION, FOR EXAMPLE.

PINK IS THE FEMININE COLOR BY DEFINITION, AND IN FRESH, CUT ROSES, SHOWS OFF COLOR GRADATIONS THAT RANGE FROM SKIN TONE TO PALE PINK, CYCLAMEN TO FUCHSIA, SHELL PINK TO CONFETTI, AND SOMETIMES EXPRESSES TENDERNESS, GRATITUDE, FRIENDSHIP AND ADMIRATION. WITH THE VARIETIES OF THIS NUANCE, *FLOWER DESIGNERS* CREATE ROMANTIC COMPOSITIONS LIKE FLOWER-CAKES, GARLANDS AND BASKETS, THE PERFECT GIFT TO CELEBRATE A BIRTH, BAPTISM OR CONFIRMATION. A COLOR THAT IS SO SENSITIVE TO FASHION, IT TURNS ALMOST PORCELAIN OR TO ANGEL SKIN IN THE VARIETIES SUCH AS AQUA GIRL, ROSALIND, ROSITA VENDELA, SECRET GARDEN, SWEET AVALANCHE OR SWEET DOLOMITI, CONFECTIONED IN BÔ PECKOUBO, HEAVEN AND REVIVAL, OLD ROSE IN PEARL AVALANCHE AND PINK TONED-DOWN TO GREEN IN ISIS, MIRANDA AND PINK FINESS.

MAUVE IS THE COLOR THAT HAS CHANGED THE WORLD. INVENTED IN A LABORATORY IN 1860 BY A YOUNG ENGLISH CHEMIST, WILLIAM PERKIN, THIS SHADE NOT ONLY BECAME A BIG TREND IMMEDIATELY (QUEEN VICTORIA WORE A DRESS OF THIS COLOR AT HER DAUGHTER'S WEDDING), IT ALSO HAD THE MERIT OF REVOLUTIONIZING THE CHEMICAL INDUSTRY, IN AN AGE IN WHICH COLORS WERE OBTAINED ONLY BY EXTRACTION FROM VEGETABLES OR ANIMALS. THIS COLOR, SO LOVED BY STYLISTS, HAS BECOME POPULAR ALSO IN THE WORLD OF FRESH CUT ROSES FOR SOME YEARS NOW. AMONG THE MOST BEAUTIFUL VARIETIES ARE AVANT GARDE, COOL WATER, DEEP WATER AND OCEAN SONG, WHICH THE MOST TRENDY FLORISTS CHOOSE ALSO FOR BRIDAL BOUQUETS AND FLORAL WEDDING DÉCOR.

THIS BOUQUET COULD, THEREFORE, BE DEDICATED TO NONE OTHER THAN SENTIMENT OR RATHER, SENTIMENTS, CREATED BY MARGHERITA ANGELUCCI, WHO MATCHED IT WITH THE PURPLE-RED OF GRAND PRIX, BABY PINK OF AQUA GIRL AND MAUVE TONES OF OCEAN SONG. THE RESULT IS AN OVERVIEW OF THE VARIETIES PRESENTED IN THIS SECTION: ROSES WITH REGAL OR PERT AIRS, BIG OR MEDIUM FLOWERS, STEMS EVEN LONGER THAN 39.3 IN (100 CM), PETALS OF TAFFETA OR VELVET THAT OPEN OUT INTO CUPS OR ROSETTES, AT TIMES EVEN SEEMINGLY SUGAR-CANDIED.

120-121 The Grand Prix roses, the Aqua Girl and the mauve Ocean Song, framed against a green crown *Asparagus* and variegated pittosphorum tobira that merge to form this romantic bouquet, designed by *Foglie, fiori e fantasia*.   122 The Fragrant Delicious rose, hybridized by the Dutch, Interplant Roses.

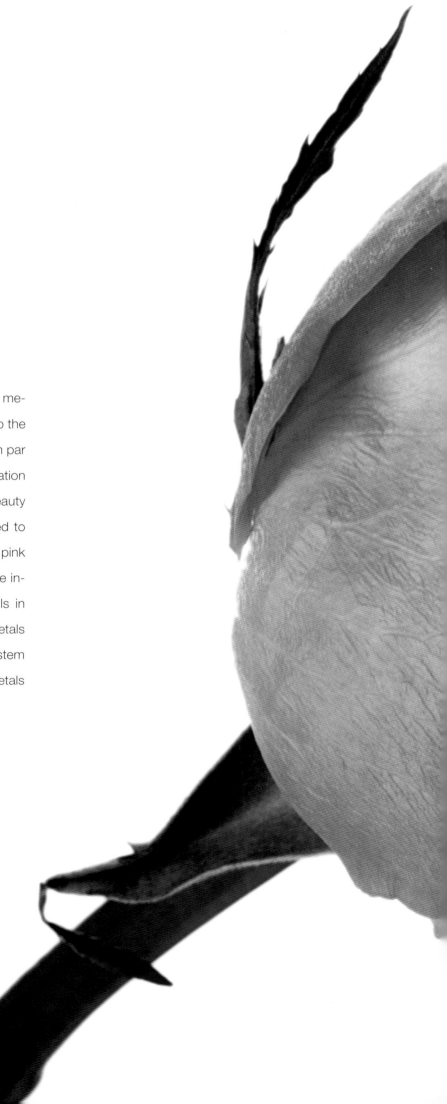

# Secret Garden

From the terraces in Babylon to the *hortus conclusus* of the medieval ages, and from the French *parterre* of André Le Nôtre to the idealistic gardens of the romantic English cottages, the garden par excellence has been the place not only for harmony, contemplation and meditation but also for pleasure and exaltation of the beauty and originality of nature. Secret Garden is precisely dedicated to the essence of the garden. A full flower of a gentle, powdery pink which is more intense on the outer petals and softened on the inner ones, this rose created by Schreurs (Netherlands) recalls in part, the other garden roses. It has a big corolla of about 30 petals which open out to measure 3.9-4.7 in (10-12 cm), on a long stem of 27.5-35.4 in (70-90 cm). The contrast of the colors of its petals against the green of its leaves is really enchanting.

# Sweet Dolomiti

Of a gentle shell-pink, this rose possesses the hues of grace, sweetness, and femininity. In a surrealistic play of color, it recalls and emanates impressions that bring to mind Venus, the Roman goddess of love and beauty, and the most famous painting of her : the *Birth of Venus*, the 13th-century work of artist, Sandro Botticelli, conserved today in the *Galleria degli Uffizi* in Florence. Gorgeous, refined, and evocative, this rose, hybridized in 2011 by the Dutch company, Olij Rozen, was honored with the Fleur Primeur title, an important recognition Flora Holland confers to the most beautiful among the new varieties presented by producers. A mutation of another famous cultivar, the Dolomiti display up to 50 petals and a stem that can reach 39.3 in (100 cm) in length.

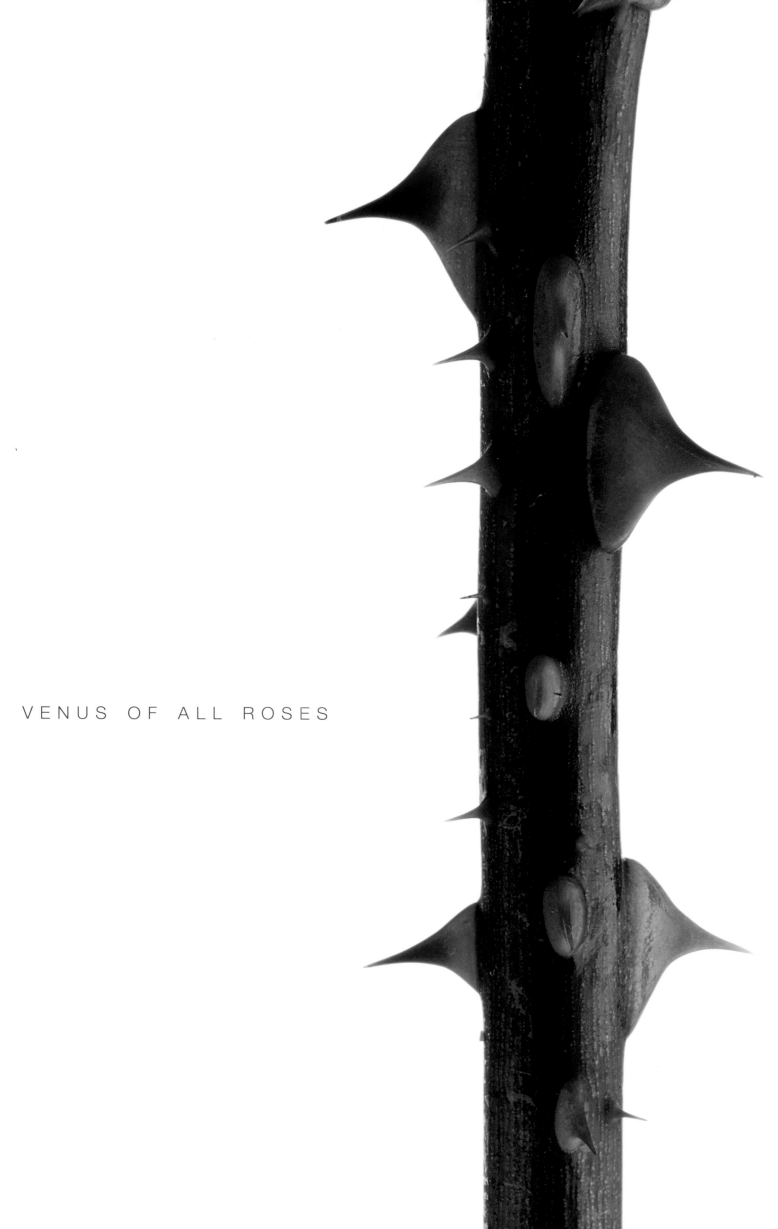

VENUS OF ALL ROSES

# Rosalind

*As you like it,* one of William Shakespeare's pastoral comedies, narrates of the vicissitudes of Rosalind who was sent into exile in the Arden Forest by her usurper uncle (Duke Frederick). She disguised herself as a boy and took the name of Ganymede, before she married Orlando. Like this heroine, woman of a thousand virtues and resources, also the Rosalind of David Austin Roses (Great Britain) is a rose full of surprises. The small cup-shaped flower of a gentle light pink, once opened accounts for an ample 165 petals and not only resembles a peony, but also emanates a mild perfume with a note of fruits. Like all the roses of David Austin, Rosalind is the fruit of long and precise research, achieved thanks to over three million in investments and 15 years of intensive cultivation.

AWESOME LIKE
SHAKESPEARE'S HEROINE

# *Avant Garde*

Stylists call mauve the grand trend of this rose, today very sought after especially for floral wedding decorations. Created by NIRP International (France), it was the muse of the young Italian wedding gown stylist, Antonio Riva, who not only drew inspiration from its hues for the gowns and accessories of his latest collections (held in high esteem in the USA, Japan and Russia), but also chose it as the flower for bouquets, table centers and place cards. Avant Garde in fact boasts interesting features : a swirl bud full of petals (about 40), a stem of 23.6-31.5 in (60-80 cm), a striking color contrast between the dark, glossy green of its leaves and the mauve of the corolla and an intense, incomparable old rose perfume.

*Taiga*

Midway between laky geranium and cherry, the color of this rose imbues gaiety and makes one recall the month of May, sunny days in the open air, excursions to the countryside, and garden parties where all is in bloom and the trees are heavy with fruit. In one word, it evokes late spring in its best period, when it preludes the summer. Hybridized by Rosen Tantau (Germany) who desired for this rose the same name as that of a historical garden cultivar (variety diffused also in Italy in the 1950s), this rose is called Taiga, in honor of the many flower enthusiasts who, especially in Eastern Europe, headed by Russia, elected it as the most beautiful flower. Cultivated in Colombia and Kenya, its flower opens out to a rosette of 2.7-3.1 in (7-8 cm), with a completely thornless stem of 19.6-27.5 in (50-70 cm).

# *Heaven*  THE FASCINATION OF SUGAR-ALMOND PETALS

According to hybridizers, pink is in reality a difficult color, too susceptible to trends and the bizarre whims of the fashion shows of Paris, Milan and New York, which season after season decree its success or failure, not only in the sector of *haute couture*. Obviously even for roses in this color, the shades are infinite, going from skin tone to fuchsia, passing through dusty powder of sugar-almonds and cyclamen, without forgetting mauve and laky geranium. The Dutch breeder, Schreurs, defied the dictates of fashion and launched Heaven in the market. With sugar-almond petals of a texture that resembles a pastry bonbon, this rose has a great bud which spreads out in a corolla of a good 40 petals and a perfectly thornless stem of 19.6-31.5 in (50-80 cm).

# *Aqua Girl*

MEDITERRANEAN EMOTION

Schreurs, the Dutch hybridizer who created this rose regards it as the "daughter" of the famous cultivar, Aqua! which evokes the month of June and Mediterranean summer. He says it makes him think not only of light at dawn, or waves that gently break over the foreshore, but also the morning dew and perfume of flowers after a storm. With pale hues that recall a baby's skin, this variety has a stem of 19.6-23.6 in (50-60 cm), completely free from thorns and a bud which explodes into a cascade of petals – even up to 55 – that are like velvet. Cultivated with success in Africa, it is most appreciated by the world's *flower designers* who choose it especially for weddings, baptisms and communions. A true and proper mini bouquet of Aqua Girl, in fact, is perfect to celebrate a newborn child.

# El Toro

Present in the myths of numberless civilizations, from the Greek to the Minoan, the bull is venerated like a god in ancient Egypt, as an emblem of strength and fertility in the Indian religion and as the symbol par excellence in Spain. The general impression in fact, of its powerful black profile does not only call to mind the corrida, arena, burning sun of August, movida and flamenco, but reminds all of just one color, that of love and passion. Red is the *capote de paseo*, the drape used by the bull fighter, as red is the costume of the flamenco dancers and also the color of this rose, hybridized by Olij Rozen (Netherlands). The rosette flower, formed with petals that seem to fluctuate to the sound of castanets, opens out to measure 2.7-3.1 in (7-8 cm), while the stem is 15.7-27.5 in (40-70 cm) long. Particularly striking is the contrast with the intense green of the leaves.

# *Pink Finess*

Almost ruffled, a bit uncombed, beautiful just the same and also sensual, Pink Finess is a flower with a strong character. Exuberant, gushing and explosive, it translates in "pink" all the qualities of the cultivar, the mythical Finess from which it originated. Hybridized by the Dutch, De Ruiter Innovations that took pleasure playing with its petals and corollas, to deceive us – with the shape and opening of the flower, since Pink Finess looks more like a peony than a rose. Its 40 petals thickly open to create a swirly, soft and fluffy round corolla. Its color merits special mention, being an almost sugar-almond pink, just ever so lightly streaked with white, and delicate water-green veins. It has a stem of 19.6-31.5 in (50-80 cm) with pretty green heart-shaped leaves and is cultivated in Europe and South America.

THIS ROSE
THINKS IT IS A PEONY

## Rosita Vendela

A mutation of the famous Vendela cultivar, this hybrid rose created by Rosen Tantau (Germany) is identical to its "sister" in many ways. For example, it has a bud of the same size and the same shape of flower, opening of the corolla and stem length. Distinct signs ? Only one, its color. The petals in fact, exhibit a fantastic type of pink. Initially however, as Rosen Tantau (Germany) recounts, this shade was not easy to achieve : in European greenhouses the pink of its corollas was not unified. So after a thousand tests and experiments, the mystery was finally solved : this rose with its rather capricious trait, loves warm climates and endows uniform tones only if cultivated in Colombia, at an altitude of over 6,561 ft (2,000 m). Rosita Vendela has beautiful green leaves.

Red Paris

LOVE AND THE COZY
ATMOSPHERE OF VILLE LUMIÈRE

If Paris, with its *quays* illuminated by night lights, its gardens, bistros and *bateaux mouches* sailing the Seine – is the archetypical city of love and lovers – at Montmartre there is a wall filled with more than 300 love messages saying "I love you" written in different languages – it is also true that the name of the "color of passion" can be given to the one and only red, as in Red Paris created by Dutch hybridizer Olij Rozen. A better name could not have been chosen for this great swirling flower of intense hues, halfway between ruby red and garnet. Red Paris has more than 30 velvety petals, and the gift of a corolla measuring 3.9-4.7 in (10-12 cm) in diameter, a stem from 19.6-35.4 in (50-90 cm) long and luxuriant green leaves. It is cultivated in Netherlands.

LOVERS' ROSE

# Passion

Red is the color of fire, love and seduction. Red on the other hand was the rose of Venus, the Roman goddess of beauty and fertility and red has always been the "red of lovers." In flower language however, each shade of color expresses different emotions and sentiments. In the same way, the cardinal red rose is a messenger of strong attraction; reddish purple expresses eternal desire. The fiery red rose incarnates the flames of passion whereas the rose with crimson petals promises solemn, eternal love. Passion, hybridized by Preesman Plants (Netherlands), is an enchanting rose with velvety petals midway between dark red and purple. The elegant corolla opens out to measure 2.7-31 in (7-8 cm), sustained by a stem 19.6-31.5 in (50-80 cm) long, and contrasts fantastically with the green of its leaves.

# Sweet Avalanche+

It was presented in Amsterdam in 2006 by Dutch hybridizer, Lex+ the Rose Factory, on the occasion of the Horti Fair, an International Gala dedicated to the world of flowers. That same year, the company won the prestigious Fleur Primeur, a sort of floral Grammy Award during which Flora Holland awards the most beautiful varieties. A mutation of the famous Avalanche+ cultivar, from which it inherited its bearing, shape, flower (the open flower measures over 4.7 in (12 cm)) and stem length (that could also reach 39.3 in (100 cm)), this rose is a favorite among *flower designers*. It is loved firstly for its vigor and productivity (it offers up to 400 stems per sq m), and then for the magnificent color of its corolla, a delicate porcelain-pink which recalls the most precious "angel-skin" coral.

## THE ROSE WITH A "PEDIGREE"

# Ocean Song

Water is an almost infinite expanse that covers three-quarters of the Earth which appears as a blue planet when seen from space. Origin of life and symbol of the force of nature, the ocean has always been the emblem of the primeval flow of vital energy which continually regenerates itself. Blown by winds and ridden by brave men who have made it the protagonist of stories, myths and legends, it is invoked also in the name of this rose cultivated by Rosen Tantau (Germany), and exhibits a delicate color between mauve and lavender, almost a melody of colors on petals that resemble satin. A big flower which measures 3.9-4.7 in (10-12 cm) when open, this rose has a stem of 19.6-31.5 in (50-80 cm) and gorgeous dark-green leaves which give a striking chromatic contrast to the shades of the corolla. It is mainly cultivated in Netherlands and South America.

## Cool Water

This rose took the name of a famous male perfume, "Davidoff Cool Water," which Zino Davidoff presents today also in the feminine version. Fresh, romantic and energizing, "Cool Water woman" blends with the notes of fruits like pineapple, watermelon and currants, and the floral aroma of the lily of the valley. The result? A perfume which in just a few drops, liberates all the essence and force of water, and waves of the sea and ocean, to perfectly exalt femininity and the beauty of modern-day women. An explosion of fresh vitality is found also in this rose created by Dutch breeder, Schreurs. Of an original pink-mauve color, it is today most appreciated in floral compositions for weddings. Cool Water has a flower of 40-45 petals that opens out to up to 4.1 in (10.5 cm). Its stem is 23.6-35.4 in (60-90 cm) long and with beautiful green leaves.

INTENSE AND FRESH VITALITY

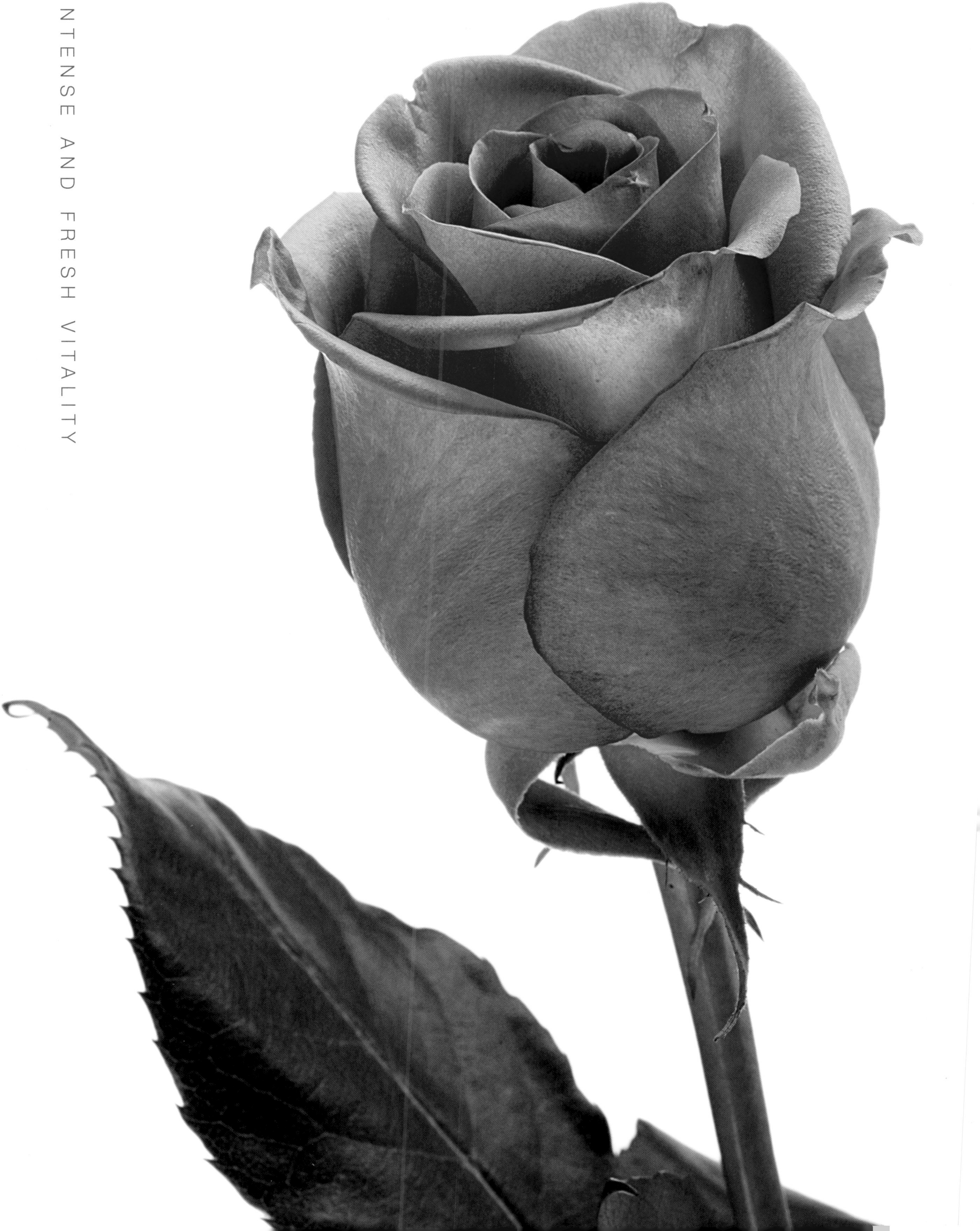

# Grand Prix

The name of this rose is a tribute to TT Assen, the motorcycle Grand Prix which has been held for over 80 years in this Dutch city. Just as the Principality of Monaco is important to Formula 1 fans, the way Wimbledon is to tennis enthusiasts, this day-long motorbike competition of all motorbike categories also offers sheer excitement to the fans of motorbike sports. Likewise, Dutch hybridizer, Terra Nigra translated these same emotions into a very beautiful red rose, a symbol of sportive passion, but above all, of love conquests. It is no surprise in fact, that this flower with its ruby petals recently superseded the historical Baccara, up to a few years ago the most marketed St. Valentine's rose. With a stem that can reach 47.2 in (120 cm) and an open corolla measuring 4.33 in (11 cm), Grand Prix is most appreciated for its dark green leaves. It is cultivated in Netherlands, France and Italy.

ROSES & MOTORS

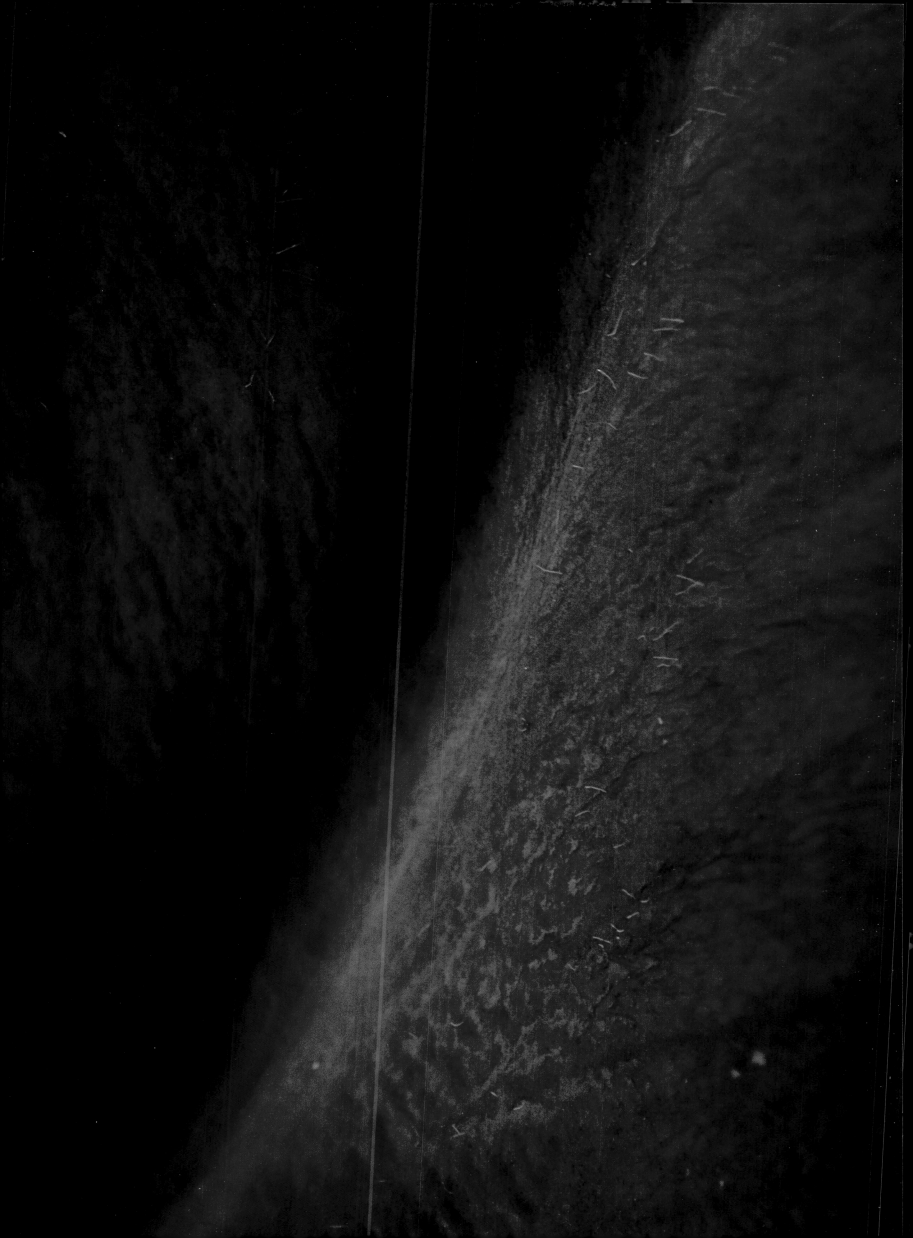

# *Miranda*

## WONDER OF WONDERS

In *The Tempest* written by William Shakespeare in 1611, Miranda is the daughter of the protagonist, Prospero, Duke of Milan. Described as a girl of rare beauty who the English dramatist himself called a *wonder*, Shakespeare even coined a new name for her : Miranda, derived from the Latin word *mirari* ("admire") and stood for "worthy of admiration." It became a common name in England only in the succeeding centuries. Just like this attractive Shakespearian girl, also the rose bred by David Austin (Great Britain) is a special flower. Besides the outer petals of a gradually toned-down shade of green and slightly curled, its heart boasts an unexpected intense pink. Its rosette flower consists of 120 petals, a 15.7-19.7 in (40-60 cm) stem and delicate fragrance of fruit.

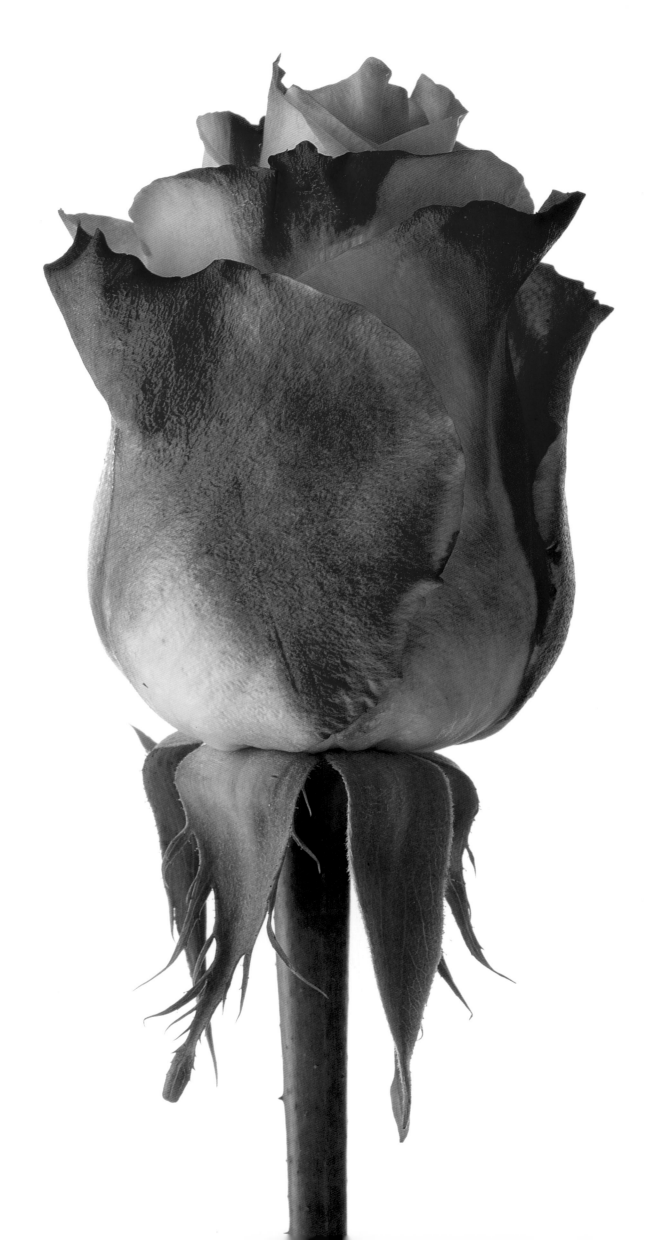

# Fragrant Delicious

A rose of many and diverse virtues, Fragrant Delicious is bewitching. This is firstly due to its sweet and intense perfume, so much like those that immediately lead you to recall the most beautiful memories, mother's cake, the rose blooming in grandma's garden, the caress of a child, the sky in spring, the first kiss... and then, because of its color, an apricot-cream with a touch of pink which becomes more intense along the borders of the petals. Crossbred by Interplant Roses (Netherlands), this rose has a good 50 petals, very few thorns and a stem that can reach 39.3 in (100 cm) in length. It blazes with color if cultivated in Ecuador, at an altitude of over 6,561 ft (2,000 m). Its creamy color thus becomes apricot and is pink, almost crimson. Its chromatic contrast is interesting, amid the dark green and gloss of its leaves, and the nuances of its corolla.

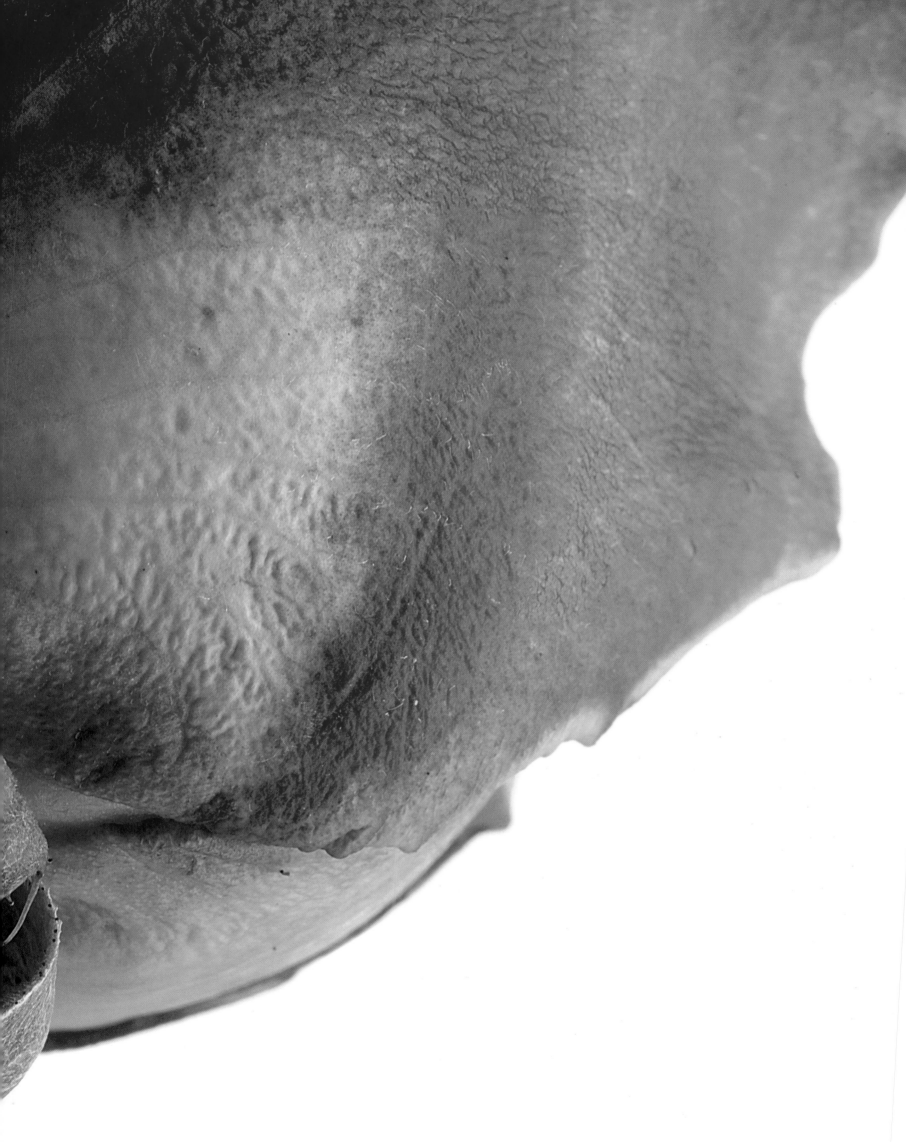

THE SWEET TRANSFORMIST

# *Matilda*

Meilland International (France) which today distributes this rose worldwide, wanted to dedicate the name of this cultivar to its Spanish breeder : Matilde Ferrer. Undoubtedly this rose took after the soil where it was created, in both colors and temperament. With a warm intense hue, an unusual terracotta red and rounded petals that make it even more special, Matilda shows off its open corolla to look like an 18th century petticoat, full of frills and flounces. A pink flower with a strong personality, it is the fruit of a painstaking crossbreeding process that produced a vigorous and productive plant, able to give at least 170 stems per sq m. Its stem is 27.5-31.5 in (70-80 cm) long.

# *Isis*

## MORE THAN A ROSE, A GODDESS

Venerated in ancient Egypt as the goddess of fertility, marriage and magic (who with her powers resuscitated her husband, Osiris), and depicted as a regal, strong and beautiful woman, the figure of Isis inspired the Dutch hybridizer, Schreurs, who chose the Greek name for this cultivar of pink flowers with green streaks. The motive of the choice ? A dual choice, says Schreurs : on one hand the beauty of this rose which when open, exhibits a pale pink which slowly intensifies, and on the other, its duration in water which lasts well beyond 20 days. Isis' flower counts up to 30 petals and a stem of 19.6-27.5 in (50-70 cm) long. It is cultivated in Netherlands, Ecuador and Kenya, where the climate and altitude (the greenhouses are usually located at over 6,561 ft (2,000 m)) render brighter hues.

# *Peckoubo*

TRIBUTE TO PINK

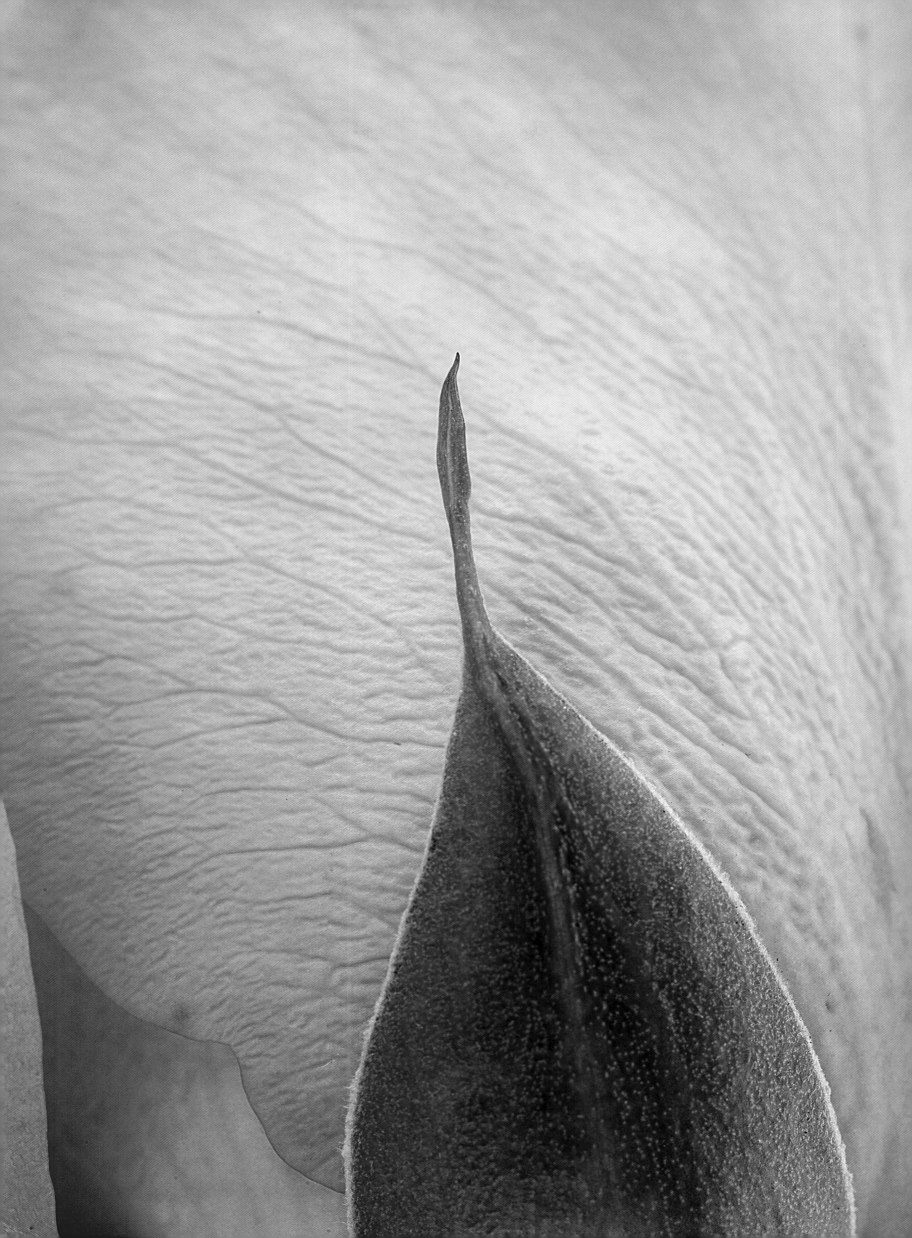

Very popular especially in Russia, this rose, also known by the name of Bõ Peckoubo and hybridized by NIRP International (France), is one of the most famous and most sold in all of Europe. Its fortune lies on one hand, in its color, an awesome full pink, pure and perfect, and on the other, in its gentle but persistent perfume. Much loved by *flower designers*, who choose it for their more romantic compositions like bouquets and floral tributes to celebrate a birth or communion, it is grown in Ecuador, Colombia and Kenya and exported to the United States and Europe. Very resistant, it has a big flower of about 4.3 in (11 cm) in diameter, is rich in petals (average of 35), with a stem that can reach 39.3 in (100 cm) in length.

# *Farfalla*

The Monarch butterflies (*Danaus plexippus*), endemic to the American continent, are famous for their migrations. Between autumn and spring they undertake a flight of over 3,106 mi (5,000 km) : starting out from North America, they reach Mexico and California, where they pass the winter, to return once again to northern regions. To pay homage to this great example of beauty and the force of nature, NIRP International, the French hybridizer created Farfalla, a rose that evokes the American butterfly not only in its cream color with orange overtones that slowly intensify, but also in its slightly frayed border, and almost fluttery petals that seem like wings. Currently grown in Kenya and Ecuador, Farfalla has a compact bud, 35 petals and a stem of 19.6-23.6 in (50-60 cm).

A HOMAGE TO BEAUTY
AND THE FORCE OF NATURE

# Red Naomi!

For the publicity launch of the Naomi! cultivar, a red rose created by Schreurs, the well informed say that the Dutch hybridizer spent a fortune. Dedicated to the famous English top model, Naomi Campbell who Schreurs wanted as special testimonial for his publicity campaign, this rose today has been flanked by two other splendid varieties, the Red and the White Naomi! Its color is an intense crimson which shades off to a darker tone, almost purple-red, and has many petals (even 75 can be counted) that seem like velvet. Romantic, sophisticated and sensual, over the last years it has been the most popular and sought after rose for St. Valentine's Day. It's corolla has an opening of 4.3-5.5 in (11-14 cm), a stem of 23.6-47.2 in (60-120 cm) and a delicate but persistent perfume.

# Deep Water

*Deep water* is the title of a documentary film which narrates the tragic story and now legend, of one of the participants of the regatta organized in 1968 by *The Sunday Times,* to repeat the astonishing feat of circumnavigating the globe alone, achieved in 1960 by Sir Francis Chichester. It was a grandiose undertaking that gave tribute to the genius, strength and perseverance of man, always challenging himself. Also this rose is a challenge to the strictest beauty standards. Hybridized by Rosen Tantau (Germany) it was named, "Deep Water," for the arduous, but highly effective combination of two different shades of pink and red, in a sole petal. A big flower with an opening of 3.9-4.7 in (10-12 cm), its stem is 23.6-31.5 in (60-80 cm) long and has wonderful green leaves.

WHEN BEAUTY CHALLENGES ITSELF

# Pearl Avalanche

Hybridized by the Dutch, Lex+ the Rose Factory, this rose is a mutation of the famous Avalanche+ cultivar, of which it conserves all the characteristics : from bearing to shape, size of the flower (which measures over 4.7 in (12 cm) when open), stem length (then even reaching 35.4 in (90 cm)), and up to a productivity of a good 400 stems per sq m. The difference lies, therefore, only in its color : a delicate and warm shade halfway between salmon and old rose, and a texture which evokes the magic and sheen of a pearl necklace. Cultivated in Netherlands, this splendid cultivar is ideal for scenographic compositions, like the grand rose created by Max van de Sluis, *flower designer* of the Dutch Royal House, who achieved this original bouquet by making use of all the petals of 15 Pearl Avalanche roses.

THE MOST PRECIOUS ROSE

A SWEET
"FLORAL SMS"

# Revival

It is a known fact that roses interpret sentiments and convey emotions. More than anything else it is their color that speaks out for them, which in flower language is synonymous to love, passion and jealousy on every occasion. So the red rose is a sort of sweet "floral message" : expressing friendship, affection and admiration. In the intense hues of Revival, for example, it is equivalent to a shy "I love U" not written on the display of a cell phone, but on the elegant corolla that opens out with a diameter of 4.7 in (12 cm). Hybridized by Rosen Tantau (Germany) in the 1990s, when pink finally returned to the limelight after a decade of oblivion, this cultivar, most appreciated by the European market, is grown in Netherlands, Germany, France, Italy and Kenya. It has a stem length of 23.6-27.5 in (60-70 cm).

# "Alphabetical index"

# "List of Hybridizers"

**David Austin Roses Ltd.**

Bowling Green Lane, Albrighton,
Wolverhampton, WV7 3HB, UK
Tel +44 (0)1902 376 300
Fax +44 (0)1902 375 177
retail@davidaustinroses.com
www.davidaustinroses.com

**De Plantis**

Pallazo Graziuso, SS 145, n. 68
80045 Pompei (NA)
Tel +39 081 861 5078
Fax +39 081 862 8081
info@deplantis.it
www.deplantis.it

**De Ruiter Innovations BV**

Meerlandenweg 55
1187 ZR Amstelveen, Netherlands
Tel +31 (0)20 6436 516
Fax +31 (0)20 6433 778
general@deruiter.com
www.deruiter.com

**Interplant Roses BV**

Broekweg 5
3956 NE Leersum, Netherlands
Tel +31 (0) 343 473 247
Fax +31 (0) 343 473 244
mail@interplant.nl
www.interplant.nl

**Kordes' Söhne Rosenschulen GmbH & Co KG**

Rosenstrasse 54
25365 Klein Offenseth-Sparrieshoop, Germany
Tel +49 (0)4121 48700
Fax +49 (0)4121 84745
info@Kordes-Rosen.com
www.gartenrosen.de

**Lex+ the Rose Factory BV**

Hoofdweg 148
1433 JX Kudelstaart, Netherlands
Tel +31 (0)297 361 422
Fax +31 (0)297 361 420
info@lex.nl
www.lex.nl

**Meilland International**

Domaine de Saint André
Le Cannet-des-Maures
83340 Le Luc-en-Provence, France
Tel +33 (0)4 7834 0034
Fax +33 (0)4 9447 9829
www.meilland.com

**NIRP International S.A.**

"Le Santa Maria" 27, Porte de France
06500 Menton, France
Tel +33 (0)4 9328 7590
Fax +33 (0)4 9328 7599
info@nirpinternational.com
www.nirpinternational.com

**Olij Rozen**

Achterweg 73
1424 PP De Kwakel, Netherlands
Tel +31 (0)297 382 929
Fax +31 (0)297 341 340
info@olijrozen.nl
www.olijrozen.nl

**Preesman Plants BV**

Aalsmeerderweg 692-694
1435 ER Rijsenhout, Netherlands
Tel +31 (0)2 9738 2200
Fax +31 (0)2 9738 2208
admin@preesman.com
www.preesman.nl

**Rosen Tantau KG**

Tornescher Weg 13
25436 Uetersen, Germany
Tel +49 (0)4122 7084
Fax +49 (0)4122 7087
tantau@rosen-tantau.com
www.rosen-tantau.com

**Schreurs BV**

Hoofdweg 81
1424 PD De Kwakel, Netherlands
Tel +31 (0)297 383 444
fleurs@schreurs.nl
www.schreurs.nl

**Terra Nigra**

Mijnsherenweg 23
1433 AP Kudelstaart, Netherlands
Tel +31 (0)297 564 116
Fax +31 (0)297 368 853
info@terranigra.com
www.terranigra.com

# "Authors' Biographies"

**Fabio Petroni** was born in Corinaldo (Ancona, Italy) in 1964, and currently lives and works in Milan. After taking up photography, he worked with the top professionals of the sector. His professional career path led him to specialize in portraits and still life, fields in which he distinguished himself for his intuitive and meticulous style. Over the years he has photographed leading celebrities in the fields of Italian culture, medicine and economics. He works with main advertising agencies and has authored numerous campaigns for prestigious, internationally renowned companies and firms. He personally handles the photographic publications of some important Italian trademarks. For White Star, he published "Horses. Master Portraits" (2010), "Mutt's Life!" (2011), "Cocktails" (2012) and "Supercats!" (2012).

**Natalia Fedeli**, born in Milan in 1959, took up studies in Psychology. In the publishing sector for twenty-seven years, she has achieved important projects for some leading Italian Publishing companies such as Mursia, Electa-Mondadori and Giorgio Mondadori Editorial. Her cultural background, personal interests and experience have always revolved around her love for nature, and all that is beautiful, two aspects she is also involved in professionally. In fact, she works for "Gardenia," the first Italian monthly magazine for plants, flowers and green lifestyles, editing the section on floral decorations, florists, flower designers and artists/craftsmen engaged in the world of greenery.

# "Acknowledgements"

The author wishes to give special thanks to Enzo Caputo of Lombardaflor (one of the major Italian importers of plants and flowers). He not only allowed his roses to be photographed for this volume, but was also a precious source of information and advice. Many thanks also go to : Margherita Angelucci of the flower shop, *Foglie, fiori e fantasia* in Milan, for her patience and precious contribution ; Maurizio Usai, landscapist and passionate garden designer, for the historical-technical information ; Charles Lansdorp, Director of the Dutch Office of flowers in Italy, who showed me around the market of fresh cut flowers as it is today, divided among cultivators, producers and auctions ; and Deborah Ghione of Nirp International, who introduced me to the hybridizing world. Thanks also to the other hybridizers I contacted, namely Georg Wieners of Rosen Tantau, Lena ter Laare of Preesman Plants, Cor den Hartog and Martin de Rooij of Lex+ the Rose Factory, Christa Boerlage of Terra Nigra, Rose Allard of Interplant Roses, Nicola Bethell and Damiano Quintili of David Austin Roses, Mirko La Galante and Laura Curti e Lara Dehen of Meilland International, Örjan Hulshof di De Ruiter Innovations, Volker Heidelbeer of W. Kordes' Söhne, Ron Egberts of Schreurs, and also Olij Rozen and Tommaso Graziuso of De Plantis.
Special thanks go also to Rosebrandt Dutch Materpiece that supplied with Lombardflor, the roses for the bouquets of *Foglie, fiori e fantasia*. Last but certainly not the least, many thanks go to Chiara Bianchi, Anna Taliento and Mario Barbaglia for their support and attentive and constructive help in proofreading the drafts.

208 Sweet Dolomiti, hybridized by the Dutch company, Olij Rozen.  Cover  Aubade, hybridized by the French company, Nirp International.  Back cover  Avant Garde, hybridized by the French company, Nirp International.

**vmb**
PUBLISHERS

VMB Publishers® is a registered trademark property of De Agostini Libri S.p.A.

© 2012 by De Agostini Libri S.p.A.
Via G. da Verrazano, 15
28100 Novara, Italy
www.whitestar.it - www.deagostini.it

Translation : Yolanda Eugenia Rillorta
Editing : Karen O'Brien

ISBN 978-88-540-2047-4

Printed in China

4  6  8  10  9  7  5  3